THE PAST IS
NEVER DEAD

THE PAST IS NEVER DEAD

THE TRIAL OF
JAMES FORD SEALE
AND MISSISSIPPI'S
STRUGGLE
FOR REDEMPTION

HARRY N. MACLEAN

BASIC
CIVITAS
BOOKS

A Member of the Perseus Books Group
New York

Library of Congress Cataloging-in-Publication Data

MacLean, Harry N.
The past is never dead : the trial of James Ford Seale and Mississippi's
struggle for redemption / by Harry N. MacLean.
p. cm.
ISBN 978-0-465-00504-8 (alk. paper)
1. Seale, James Ford—Trials, litigation, etc. 2. Trials (Kidnapping)—
Mississippi. 3. Trials (Murder)—Mississippi. 4. Ku Klux Klan (1915–)
5. African Americans—Crimes against—Mississippi—History—
20th century. 6. African Americans—Civil rights—Mississippi.
7. Mississippi—Race relations. 8. Racism—Mississippi. 9. Redemption—
Political aspects—Mississippi. I. Title.
KF225.S43M33 2009
345.762'0254—dc22   2009019241

For my brother
Michael Galleher MacLean

The past is never dead. It's not even past.

— WILLIAM FAULKNER,
Requiem for a Nun

ACT I

ACT I

The frail old man enters the courtroom not in an orange jumpsuit and shackles, as in days past, but in pressed slacks and a gray button-down dress shirt. He steadies himself on the lectern before sitting down at the defense table, where he receives a pleasant smile from his female attorney. The elegant and grandly elevated black judge directs the marshals to seat the jury. Eight whites and four blacks walk in and take their seats with great solemnity. On the screen in front of them, and right in the elderly man's face, the photos of two young black men flash. The audience waits with anticipation for the curtain to rise on the latest act in Mississippi's great morality play.

To date, each Klansman brought into court for long-past crimes against blacks in Mississippi has gone down and gone down hard: Byron De La Beckwith, convicted for the murder of Medgar Evers (third trial); James Caston, Charles Caston, and Hal Crimm, convicted of manslaughter in the murder of a one-armed sharecropper, Rainey Pool (first trial); Ernest Avants, convicted for the murder of Ben Chester White (second trial); Edgar Ray Killen, convicted of manslaughter in the deaths of Michael Schwerner, Andrew

Goodman, and James Chaney (second trial); Imperial Wizard Sam Bowers, convicted for the murder of Vernon Dahmer (second trial).

Now, here, today, May 31, 2007, the eighth defendant sits quietly, almost peacefully, in the dock. James Ford Seale, age seventy-one but looking well into his eighties, is on trial for the first time for the kidnapping and murder of two young black men in Franklin County, Mississippi, in the spring of 1964.

When the bottom half of Charles Moore's body was found hung up on a log by a fisherman in a back chute of the Mississippi River thirty miles north of Natchez on July 12, 1964, over 250 FBI agents were in Mississippi on J. Edgar Hoover's direct orders, scouring the countryside for Schwerner, Goodman, and Chaney, the three civil rights workers who had disappeared after being released from jail in Neshoba County on June 21. The common belief was that the feds were there in force because two of the missing three were white men from New York. In fact, when the cops first recovered Moore's body, they got excited about the possibility that it could be one of the three civil rights workers—the *M* on the belt buckle might stand for Michael Schwerner—and quickly phoned the FBI and authorities in Neshoba County. Law enforcement and the national media hustled eagerly to the river, only to be disappointed when the body turned out to be one of the missing black youths from Franklin County.

Five months ago, Seale, a former crop duster, truck driver, and town cop, was living out his days peacefully in a motor home on his step-daughter's property in Roxie, a small town in the heart of Southwest Mississippi. Then the feds swooped down in the middle of a winter night and cuffed him away. For years, the papers had reported him dead, and he's so ill now, he still might die an unconvicted man, like all of his alleged coconspirators, except for one. Squirreled away in the historic Edison Walthal down the block is Charles Marcus Edwards, Seale's fellow Klansman, waiting to testify against him.

Nowhere is the power of the past to configure the present in Mississippi more evident than in this case. A diminutive black woman with streaks of gray in her hair glances at former FBI agent Jim Ingram in the back of the courtroom and whispers to the person seated next to her, "Oh, Lord, I remember him. FBI, we had to keep an eye on them too. I wouldn't trust him even now." Ingram, age seventy-five and a towering six feet, four inches, is a legend from the days of the great struggle. He greets many of the people entering the courtroom as old friends.

The woman, L. C. Dorsey—Dr. L. C. Dorsey now, although she seldom uses the title—shakes her head at how strange it still seems for the state to prosecute a Klansman for killing two black men. She remembers a far different time. When she was a girl on a plantation in the Delta, a black boy named Odell was known to have a crush on a white girl. One day he simply disappeared, and nobody ever said a word about it. Another time, rumors reached her father that a white woman in town had her eye on one of Dorsey's brothers. Her father, knowing the mere rumor put his son's life in jeopardy, stuck him on a bus to Detroit the very next morning. Back then, words or looks could get you killed.

Ingram remembers how things were back then as well. The FBI was the law, the law was white, and white was dangerous. He worked most of the big cases, starting with Schwerner, Goodman, and Chaney (known in Mississippi as the Neshoba County case or the case of the three civil rights workers, and frequently referred to in the national media as the *Mississippi Burning* case), and he helped convict Edgar Ray Killen in the Neshoba County murders and Sam Bowers, the head of the White Knights of the Ku Klux Klan, in the murder of Vernon Dahmer, the head of the Hattiesburg NAACP who burned to death in 1966 when the Klan firebombed his home. Ingram went on to glory as the deputy director of the FBI and, after retiring from the bureau, became director of public safety for Mississippi. The state brought him out of retirement for the second prosecution of Killen in 2004, and now the feds have brought him back for Seale. Ingram sees a serious problem with this case; in all the other prosecutions, there was a previous trial transcript, but not here. Many of the witnesses are either dead or almost dead. The government has only one man: Charles Marcus Edwards.

There could have been two defendants in the case: James Ford Seale and the state of Mississippi. Seale for kidnapping and murder and Mississippi for complicity—knowingly aiding and abetting, conspiring with, fathering, and furthering James Ford Seale. The subtext in this play is almost more powerful than the story: Mississippi trying to claw its way out of the devil's pit in its drive for acceptance in the civilized world. Mississippi well knows the truth of itself: it is not only the Deep South, it is the Deepest South—home of Jefferson Davis, president of the Confederacy; second state to join the Confederacy, last to ratify the Thirteenth Amendment abolishing slavery (1995), and first to ratify the Eighteenth Amendment prohibiting liquor (1918); site of the highest number of reported lynchings in the Confederate states (539 from 1882 to 1966; Georgia was close behind, with 492). Even the other ten Confederate states look down on Mississippi, the unreconstructed, unrepentant, and unloved stepsibling. Mississippi knows that outside its borders there appears to be near unanimity that it is a lousy place. As New York Congressman Charlie Rangel famously put it, "Mississippi gets more federal money than it gives, but who would want to live in Mississippi anyway?"

It's not as if Mississippi doesn't already feel bad about the past or tries to justify or even explain it, at least not publicly. Mississippi wants out, and it wants in; it wants freedom. But the people here know there's no sense in changing things just to please others, like dropping the Stars and Bars from the state flag or abolishing the celebration of Confederate Decoration Day. Your past is your past, after all, just as you are who you are. One thing you can do, though, is prosecute race murderers from the sixties. Mississippi got the train rolling in 1994 with its successful prosecution of De La Beckwith, and in 2007 it leads with seven of the twenty-two convictions in the Confederate states to its credit.

The small man with the large forehead, sitting upright and unmoving at the defense table, is the latest stone on Mississippi's path to redemption. The path is fraught with perils for both sides, and both sides are acutely aware of them. The prosecution is worried about closet racists—those who have learned the correct language but still harbor the old sentiments. The prosecution is also worried about the native Mississippian who resents the way the world looks at the state, who takes the thin-lipped, squinty-eyed, down-in-the holler Hollywood image personally and doesn't want a thing to do with playing up to the hypocrites from the North.

For the defense, the worry is that regardless of the facts, Seale is destined to be the eighth straight sacrifice on the road to redemption. Who, black or white, wants to sit on the first jury in these recent cases to acquit a Klansman of killing a black? Some say that it might well be as impossible to acquit a white man of killing a black man today as it would have been to convict a white man of killing a black man forty-three years ago.

Chapter 2

Mississippi Burning (from the FBI acronym MIBURN) was Hollywood's version of the killing of the three civil rights workers in Neshoba County in June 1964. Gene Hackman plays the role of the rogue but heroic FBI agent; Willem Dafoe plays his handsome, sensitive, and youthful FBI boss; sexy Frances McDormand plays the wife of a murderous Klansman/deputy sheriff. The movie depicts a land of ignorant and violent whites who are obsessed with burning churches and houses and beating and lynching blacks. Not one of them, save the deputy's wife, who sleeps with Hackman to preserve her little shred of humanity, has a heart or a conscience. The blacks are shown for the most part as cowardly victims unwilling or unable to interrupt their own fates. It's the white men from the North who show up and save the day. The flames, the sex, the stars, the violence played out in the wooded rolling hills of Neshoba County—America loved it: That's Mississippi. And it's not us. And the truth is, to the rest of the world, that still is Mississippi. So Mississippians believe others believe, and they're not wrong. *Mississippi Burning* loops endlessly in the cultural mind of America.

The lead prosecutor in the Seale case is Paige Fitzgerald, a slender woman in her early forties from the Justice Department in Washington. Fitzgerald cut her teeth on Klan murder cases in Mississippi a few years ago when she put Ernest Avants away for life for the 1963 murder of Ben Chester White, an elderly black sharecropper. Avants, like De La Beckwith and Killen, preened with unrepentance at his trial—unlike the elderly man in slacks and pressed shirt sitting quietly at the counsel table, who by appearance and manner could be a retired history teacher.

Fitzgerald's vivacious smile and gracious manner fools no one. She has an icy brilliance, a knife's edge of focused relentlessness that can't be passed off as the usual prosecutorial vigor. She is considered highly opinionated by many on the prosecution's side and downright mean by others. Some in law enforcement suspect her of being antipolice, perhaps because she has prosecuted several Mississippi cops for civil rights violations. But U.S. Attorney Dunn Lampton had watched her nail Avants in 2003, and he wanted her to help do the same to Seale.

As Fitzgerald interrogates potential jurors, she is worried about *Mississippi Burning*, and she's also worried about the movie *Ghosts of Mississippi*, the story of the 1995 trial of De La Beckwith for the murder of Medgar Evers. A maniacal James Woods plays De La Beckwith wonderfully, and Alec Baldwin plays the hero, local assistant district attorney Bobby Delaughter. That trial was the first scene in the first act of the redemption drama not just for Mississippi but also for the entire South. Maybe now, twelve years later, jurors might think, Enough is enough. Why should we put Mississippi through this all over again? Here we have an obviously sick old man who might have done something bad forty-three years ago, but he's led a good life since then, and what good is it going to do to put him—us, Mississippi, the country—through the trauma all over again?

If you push guilt or shame hard enough on someone and make them feel bad enough, they might just say fuck you and the horse you rode in on; in this case, the one you rode in on from Washington, D.C. Deep in the soul of Mississippi lingers the idea—still, to this day—that the federal government is the real culprit in the endless turmoil that began with the Civil War, followed by Reconstruction (which only enfranchised the black male), then *Brown vs. Board of Education* (authored, as one Mississippi judge put it, by the Supreme Court of Sociology), the Freedom Riders, the admission of James Meredith to Ole Miss at the point of thousands of federal bayonets (ordered there by President Kennedy), and finally Freedom Summer, and the civil rights laws of the sixties. Violence might be the wrong way to handle the problems, and blacks deserved equal rights, but Mississippi was their home; they belonged to Mississippi.

One juror, when queried by the prosecution on his feelings about the northerners on the government team, surveyed the prosecution table and noted with a raised brow that by his count only two of the four lawyers seated there were locals. Even the judge smiled at this.

Questioning of the prospective jurors reveals that most of them have indeed seen *Mississippi Burning*, some have seen *Ghosts of Mississippi*, and a few have seen *4 Little Girls*, a documentary about four black girls killed in the bombing of a church in Birmingham, Alabama, in 1963. Most understand that *Mississippi Burning* reflects the way the outside world sees Mississippi.

CHAPTER 3

In his time, Martin Luther King Jr. saw Mississippi as the most dangerous place in the South. Willie Morris wrote in 1981 that many Americans remain afraid of Mississippi. To this day, most northerners have never been to Mississippi, and few have any plans to go there. Some say they would hesitate to drive through Mississippi with out-of-state plates or wonder if they might need a passport to get in and out. Tongue-in-cheek perhaps, but not totally. The truth is that the rest of the county doesn't really care about Mississippi. To most Americans, Mississippi is a place in our country but not of our country, a place with odd customs and traditions, a place stuck in the past, in the *Mississippi Burning* past, a culture frozen in amber, fiery crosses and all.

If civilization does exist in Mississippi, the view from up North goes, it will most likely be found in Oxford or Natchez. But Natchez was a major marketplace for slaves, and the wealth of its magnificent cotton plantations was built on their backs. And Oxford is home to Ole Miss, the soul of the white ruling aristocracy, which rioted to prevent a black man from enrolling. Faulkner might have been from Oxford, but he himself was never free from the agony and paradoxes of a segregated society.

The natives, the view holds, are ignorant and utterly unrepentant. It's as if it's still 1964, and all Mississippi—every village, every farm, every crossroads—is Neshoba County. It's *Mississippi Burning* played out as real; it's the fight over the Stars and Bars on the state flag; it's the horrible litany of statistics placing Mississippi at the bottom of every measure of a healthy civilization: most obese, highest rate of teen pregnancy, lowest education level, lowest per capita income, highest rate of venereal disease, highest infant mortality rate, and on and on. (One list in particular displays the media's almost endemic, and sometimes irrational, antipathy toward Mississippi: *Self* magazine ranks Jackson as the worst city in the country for a healthy sex life because it has only one abortion clinic.) A scholar might go there to study the inhabitants and their customs, as one might an indigenous tribe in Brazil.

Beaten down by this almost universal attitude, Mississippi has lost its voice, and the little squawks that might issue forth sound defensive or whiney. Mississippi could point out that it has more black elected officials than any other state in the Union, but it doesn't bother—someone would point out that it doesn't have, and hasn't had, a black elected to state-level official since Reconstruction. Mississippians understand only too well that the past is never the past. (The most common misquotation of Faulkner's pronouncement, "The past is never dead. It's not even past.")

In fact, Mississippi is strikingly beautiful and incredibly diverse, a land of seashores and pine-covered hills, wide bayous and slow-flowing rivers, and a broad, seemingly endless alluvial plain bounded by a mighty river. The urban areas seem typically American. Billboards contain the usual warnings about drug use and teen pregnancy. Palm trees don't line the airport runways, jeeps carrying AK-47-toting guards don't pull up along side your plane as it taxis to a stop, the signs in the concourses are in English, and you don't have to pass through customs. The locals are courteous and friendly—in fact, quite friendly: if you ask a question, you could easily find yourself in a five-minute conversation.

At the hotel, where all three of the desk employees are black, the manager decides that an out-of-state visitor should have one of the nicer suites. He gives out a code for the wireless Internet in the room, which is clean and well furnished. The bed is firm. The TV has cable. Free breakfast from 6 to 10 A.M. This is America.

After you've spent a little time here, though, the place begins to remind you of an attractive woman with an unsavory past who's trying to go straight but keeps coming across men who knew her back when. Dress her up, fix her hair, teach her good grammar, but you'll always wonder what lingers inside.

But isn't America the land of second chances? Remember former Alabama Klansman Justice Hugo Black, who became a leading voice on the liberal Warren Court and former Klansman Senator Robert Byrd of West Virginia, who became a respected constitutional scholar in the U.S. Senate? Why not Mississippi? Why not James Ford Seale?

If you stay around long enough, you'll find yourself seduced by the ineluctable paradox that is Mississippi. You'll come to accept that you'll never get your head around it, that the ironies are endless—like the fact that Elvis Presley's unique sound derives from a white man singing like a black man—and that all you can really do is peel back a layer here and there, poke around a bit, and absorb what you can. Still, in spite of that, in stray moments of particular lucidity, you imagine that you will one day see through the profusion of nuances and conflicts and subtleties and contradictions and inconsistencies and incongruities to some new truth, some harmonious undergirding that will make sense of this place and its past. So you keep on trying.

CHAPTER 4

Mississippi, despite its homogeneity in the eyes of the rest of the country, is a land of many faces. Jackson, the capital, named after Andrew Jackson, sits on a bluff overlooking the Pearl River in almost the dead center of Mississippi. Occupied twice and burned three times by Union troops during the Civil War (once by Gen. William Tecumseh Sherman)—thus earning the name "Chimneyville"—Jackson has around 176,000 people (350,000 in the metropolitan area). The city is home to seven colleges and universities, the University Medical Center, a symphony and performing arts center, an art museum, and an international airport (recently renamed, after much delicate negotiation, the Jackson-Evers [for Medgar Evers] International Airport). The city is about 70 percent black and 30 percent white, with a black mayor and a majority-black city council. Charges of corruption and malfeasance in city government are everyday events. The mayor is on trial in federal court for running a vigilante operation against alleged drug dealers. Violent crime is rampant. Most of Jackson's schools are de facto segregated, due in large part to ongoing white flight to the suburbs. The black middle class is also fleeing the inner city.

Other Mississippians often refer to people in north-eastern Mississippi towns like Tupelo, Elvis's birthplace, as "hill people." This area, the northern area of what is known as the Piney Woods, was never cleared for cotton. It has a black population of roughly 20 percent.

Although not a major area of slaveholders, northeastern Mississippi was the scene of several major battles in the Civil War. At the Battle of Corinth, a few miles south of Shiloh, the victorious Union army established control of the hub of major Confederate rail lines running north and south. At Brice's Crossroads, north of Tupelo, Gen. Nathan Bedford Forrest, infamous for his execution of black soldiers at Fort Pillow and a founder of the Ku Klux Klan after the war, furthered his legend by defeating a Union force twice the size of his own. Confederate general Earl Van Dorn, a dashing womanizer, destroyed a massive Union supply depot at the town of Holly Springs—only to be shot and killed later as he sat at his desk by a cuckolded husband—forcing Gen. U. S. Grant to delay his critical campaign against Vicksburg. The eventual fall of Vicksburg split the Confederacy in half and opened the Mississippi, causing President Lincoln to rejoice that "the Father of Waters again goes unvexed to the sea."

Today, northeastern Mississippi seems not that dissimilar from the days of the war: gently winding roads; wooded, rolling hills with patches of crops here and there; farmhouses and ponds set back from the road; green squares speckled with cows; small cemeteries fenced in wrought iron; wooden trestles over exotic-sounding rivers like Buttahatchee and Luxapilla Creek, which probably carried gray troops on the march to battle, or perhaps in retreat; clapboard churches with shining white spires, the preacher's simple home a few yards away; lowlands too wet to plant but good for hunting. And still very few people.

The rolling hills come to an end in the east at the Appalachian Mountains and in the west at the Yazoo River (an Indian name meaning "River of the Dead"), the eastern rim of Paul Simon's "national guitar," the Delta, an ironed-flat swath of land roughly 150 miles long and 50 miles wide, ending at the Mississippi riverbank towns, such as Clarksdale and Greenville, many of which were devastated by the catastrophic flood of 1927, when Big River, as William Faulkner called it, jumped its banks.

The rest of the state shakes its head over the Delta. About 80 percent black and with eighteen mostly black towns, the Delta is terribly poor. You hear it called a Third World country, or Mississippi's Mississippi, or a rural ghetto. Impressive to a southerner, or even an easterner, because of its impeccable flatness, to someone from the center of the country it's reminiscent of the farmlands of Kansas and Nebraska. These days, you even see fields of winter wheat, corn, and soybeans. Flooded over thousands of years by the Mississippi, it contains some of the world's richest soil, yet is inhabited by some of the country's poorest people. When you leave the highways and drive through the neighborhoods of small towns like Itta Bena and Tutwiller, you encounter a seemingly irreversible dilapidation of the land and spirit.

After the dense, swampy forest was cleared in the early 1800s, slaves were brought from Virginia and the Carolinas to create and work the great plantations. After the Civil War, some blacks left for the North, although many

stayed and sharecropped the plantations. When mecha-
nization hit the plantations in the fifties, jobs in the fields
began disappearing. Blacks migrated either to the towns
or to the North. The few factories around pulled out. The
large towns, like Clarksdale, Greenville, and Greenwood,
are now majority black. The downtowns of many communities have been reduced to broken sidewalks, vacant
storefronts, and an occasional bus station or bar. Today,
27 percent of the families in the Delta live below the
poverty line. The black kids go to the public schools, and
the white kids attend private schools. Half of the kids in
the pubic schools drop out before graduation.

Before the Civil War, Mississippi was perhaps the
wealthiest state in the Union, based mainly on cotton
production. After the war, with the destruction of the
slave-system plantations—most capital in Mississippi was
invested in land and slaves, and when the latter suddenly
disappeared from the books, the value of the former
plummeted—it soon became the poorest.

Today, Mississippi is gaining steam economically.
Northrop Grumman Ship Systems on the Gulf Coast provides thousands of jobs. Nissan has a major factory in Can-
ton (4,000 jobs), and Toyota has plans to open a large plant
in Tupelo, formerly a furniture-manufacturing community
(4,000 jobs.) The John Stennis Space Center in southern
Mississippi builds engines for spacecraft. Gulfport is the
third largest container-shipping port in the country. But,
other than extensive catfish farms, a Viking Corporation
plant and luxury hotel in Greenwood, and a few casinos on
the riverboats and the Indian reservations, there are no
economic gems in the Delta. One local politician says that

outside businessmen have the perception that the Delta is "too black and that means too union and bad schools."

Along the southern edge of the state runs the Gulf Coast: Biloxi and Gulfport, a few artists communities like Bay St. Louis, and miles of man-made beaches. The Gulf Coast, dominated by the fishing industry for centuries, settled by the French and Spanish and traded back and forth between them for years—and therefore with a large Catholic population—seems more like Louisiana than Mississippi. Because of the seafood industry, the area has become a conglomeration of French, Spanish, Yugoslavs, Cambodians, Vietnamese, and Mexicans, which, the locals claim, has resulted in a more tolerant attitude.

Gulf Coast whites proudly point out that the Klan never really got a foothold in the region, which is about 20 percent black. That's not the whole story: in 1960 a group of whites attacked 125 blacks, including women and children, with chains, clubs, and lead pipes as they attempted to use the segregated Biloxi beaches, resulting in a series of "wade-ins" and, eventually, federal intervention.

The Gulf Coast has a long and vivid history of corrupt government and gangsterism, initially based on bootlegging, prostitution, and gambling. Tourism and gaming were becoming the draws before Katrina, which tore the coast up and resulted in the loss of 16,000 local jobs. People in the Delta and the Piney Woods often refer to the people in these parts as "coastal trash."

Even years after Katrina, the coast still feels like a wasteland, with empty waterfronts, miles of bare cement pads where houses used to be, and garish, boxy casinos. Of the many antebellum homes along the coast, Jefferson

Davis's plantation home, Beauvoir House, is one of the few left standing, although it was badly damaged.

People from all over the state—and there are slightly under 3 million inhabitants (only 1.8 percent of whom are Hispanic, as opposed to a national figure of 14.8 percent)—are quick to point out how unfairly Mississippi was treated, as usual, in the national media after Katrina. The stories all talked about New Orleans, Louisiana. You'd think the storm had just scraped a little sand off coastal Mississippi. The fact is, Mississippians insist, you didn't hear as much about the damage and trauma here because Mississippi did a much better job of dealing with the hurricane and taking care of its people, and that just wasn't news, not coming out of Mississippi. It's that pride thing; you find it everywhere in Mississippi, among whites and blacks, rural and urban, old and young. It's not just defensive either; it's genuine. It's a mysteriously beveled fit with the imponderable moral burden the state shoulders.

CHAPTER 5

The U.S. Southern District of Mississippi covers forty-five counties and extends all the way to the Gulf Coast, so sitting in the jury pool are rural and city folks, young and old, employed and not, and, of course, black and white. Missing are the commercial class, the bankers and dentists and lawyers, all apparently too busy to participate in the workings of justice. Judge Henry Wingate, Mississippi's first and only black federal judge, appointed by Ronald Reagan, had, over the vigorous objections of the defense, sent out a lengthy questionnaire to potential jurors probing racial attitudes; he asked if they had seen *Mississippi Burning* and what they thought of it, whether they or anyone in their family had been members of the Klan, and what they thought were the causes of racial unrest. So prospective jurors knew what was coming before they even reached the courthouse, and many of them want nothing to do with the case. A surprise is the amount of violence and illness in the people's lives, and their willingness to talk about intimate details in front of strangers.

Seale has a way of holding his chin in and his chest out, like he's at attention, when he walks. His head is oddly shaped; his features are gathered more on the bottom half of his face, leaving an empty forehead, exaggerated by near baldness. In his 1964 booking photo, he resembled James Dean: hair waved and slicked back, a slight surliness touching his mouth, seductive eyes. (Charles Edwards's booking photo shows him with a cocked left eye, and he looks either dull witted or extremely loaded.) Seale is smaller than his primary lawyer, Kathy Nester, who jokingly refers to herself as Rubenesque.

Nester is a dedicated liberal and former civil rights lawyer. She admits she doesn't know what happened in Franklin County on May 2, 1964, but she is adamant that the government has no case against her client. If he were accused of anything other than being a Klansman who had kidnapped two black men, the government would never have brought charges. It's set up to be a Klan trial, a chance for the jury to renounce the hated Klan, to make someone—Seale—pay for the sins of the state, and to distance themselves from the past as well, to prove that they are not racists. The government wants Seale badly, but they're going to have to come through her to get him.

In the courtroom, the judge's staff is predominantly black; the potential jurors are more white than black; the chief marshal is black; the lawyers, with one exception, are white; the audience is significantly more black than white. You notice these things because, after all, the trial is about race. In Mississippi, everything is about race sooner or later.

Prior to the great migration of blacks to the North in the forties and fifties, Mississippi had more black than white citizens, as did most southern states. Now, Mississippi has the highest percentage of blacks—36 percent—of any state. The impossible quest for jurors who are unaffected by race, or who are affected but can put the affect aside, gets off to a dramatic start when an elderly black man takes the stand and says flat out he thinks Seale is guilty. Being here has stirred things up. He was at church one Sunday back then, when the preacher called out, "Run! Run!"

"I ran for my life, and we all got out before the bomb went off, blowing things up from the entrance to the pulpit."

He pauses.

"They rode through and shot up our houses, and we had to cut the lights off and stay away from the windows and out of the yard. Those things have come back now, and they make me feel he's guilty, and I couldn't deny it."

The matter-of-fact truth of the story jolts the courtroom: that's simply the way it was, and this is the way he is, and that's it.

A white woman from rural Mississippi says she suffers from clinical depression and has twice tried to kill herself. She couldn't concentrate enough to follow the trial. "I'm probably brain dead," she says in another burst of matter-of-fact honesty. Another white woman says she's an alcoholic and she hasn't had her first drink of the day, but she's thinking about it right as she sits here in the chair. An attitude is becoming apparent among the prospective jurors: If you want me, this is what you get. If you don't want me, fine, I'll go home.

Some of the prospective jurors want out of jury duty badly. A young, attractive white woman is wearing a "Southern Girl" T-shirt with a Confederate battle flag license plate on the back. She begs off, claiming she's the only caretaker of a bedridden father. A one-armed chicken farmer says he's got three chicken houses, a $70,000 note, and no help. One white woman is shaking on the stand and claims she is suffering an anxiety attack at the very moment. When asked if she can handle the trial, she says, "Don't much look like it." She also doubts the wisdom of going after old men for old crimes. "I just feel like God's gonna be the punishment in the end."

God is a central player. A white woman declares forcefully that she couldn't reach a verdict because only God can judge. A black truck driver claims he knows nothing about the case; he doesn't watch TV and on the road he only listens to gospel music. Even the judge mentions his Catholic upbringing during questioning.

A middle-aged white woman says that she was a teenager growing up outside of Philadelphia when the three civil rights workers were killed. She is pleased Edgar Ray Killen was convicted for the crimes, and she is glad Seale got arrested for these murders. This trial is bringing back old feelings about the murder of those three boys, and she's sure the defendant is guilty.

The judge works on her: Could you put your feelings aside and consider the case based only on the facts? Unlike some others, the woman carefully considers the question. How do you put your feelings aside? You can say you will, but can you? I'm a fair person, she says, but feelings you have when you're young don't change, and they're bound to come up in the trial. She's also quite aware of how the rest of the country looks at Mississippi. Maybe making Klansmen pay for the past will show the world Mississippi isn't such a bad place after all.

Portraits of past federal judges decorate the courtroom walls. One of them, Judge Harold Cox, might be gazing down on these proceedings with some pride; it was in his courtroom in Meridian that seven of the eighteen defendants in the Neshoba County trial were convicted of conspiracy charges in the murder of the three young men, no mean accomplishment in Mississippi in 1967. Former FBI agent Jim Ingram remembers Cox as a fair and demanding judge and is convinced he was never a racist. To "movement" people, black and white civil rights workers in the '60s, and Mississippi liberals of today, he was a judicial racist. Appointed by President Kennedy at the insistence of Senator James "Big Jim" Eastland, he will be noted in history for calling black plaintiffs in a voter-registration case "a bunch of chimpanzees." He is reported to have said, after imposing sentences of three to ten years on the defendants in the Neshoba County case, "They killed one nigger, one Jew, and a white man. I gave them all what I thought they deserved." Yet he gradually ended up supporting the government's position in many civil rights and public accommodations cases. Like Mississippi itself, he changed, or appeared to change, with the times.

The wooden benches in the courtroom are curved awkwardly, making for a painful sit after a few hours. The room is freezing cold, as are many buildings in Mississippi, perhaps to compensate for the sweltering summer heat. From the tall ceiling hang eight brass-rimmed half globes, throwing off a sharp glint of federal majesty. On the wall behind the judge, hidden behind a curtain of blue velvet, is a colorful mural constructed by the WPA showing blacks working in a field of cotton. That the mural has been hidden and not removed altogether seems somehow fitting for Mississippi. Judge Wingate has been known to pull back the curtain and tell visitors the history of the painting.

During jury selection, the first three or four rows of benches behind the prosecution table are mainly filled with blacks. Thomas Moore, the brother of Charles Eddie Moore, who stirred up the case in 1998, sits in the first row, next to his twenty-six-year-old son, Jeffrey, who bears a remarkable resemblance to his uncle Charles. In the same row sits Thelma Collins, sister of Henry Hezekiah Dee, who was hustled out of town not long after her brother's body was found and who has lived her life in Chicago.

Thomas Moore bears a look of implacable sorrow on his heavy brow. He made a promise to his mother not to seek vengeance for the death of his brother, Charles— she didn't want to lose her only remaining child—and to get on with his life. He kept that promise for thirty-four years, until the day in 1998 when he read about a black man being dragged to his death in Jasper, Texas. You don't see anger or vengeance in his eyes now; you see instead a quest for recognition of his brother's life and a profound desire to have the weight of guilt and shame lifted from his shoulders.

On the other side of the aisle, behind the defense table, the benches are empty. Although Seale has one son, two daughters, and numerous grandchildren, none has showed up. One prospective black juror said that she felt bad for Seale after seeing him on television in his orange jumpsuit and protective vest. Maybe the defense is going to play it that way: dying old man all alone, abandoned by his family and ganged up on by the federal government. It didn't work for Killen, who was in a wheelchair and hooked up to oxygen.

A middle-aged black woman declares with conviction that she could never be fair to the defendant. She believes Seale is guilty. She sees not a hint of remorse on his face. When reminded by the judge that at this stage of the proceedings the defendant has nothing to be remorseful about because he has denied the charge and is presumed innocent, she makes her position perfectly clear. "I have a racist attitude," she says. "I'm fifty years old, and I grew up with this stuff, and I've been treated badly because of the color of my skin. To be honest, I couldn't put that aside. I'm a racist."

It isn't a confession: she doesn't seem to feel particularly bad about her attitude. Nor is it a claim of victimhood. It's just a simple statement of honest, unalterable fact. A long pause follows for everyone to consider the notion that here in Mississippi, a black can consider herself a racist. The judge dismisses her.

A young black woman testifies that she lives in Roxie, just down the road from Seale. Everyone in the black community thinks he's guilty of murder, so she figures he must be. Dismissed.

Chapter 6

Franklin County, named for Benjamin Franklin, lies in the heart of Southwest Mississippi. The land is farm country, with only three "statutory towns" and fewer than 8,000 people. Nearly half of the county consists of the Homochitto National Forest (pronounced "Hamachitta" by the locals). Heading south out of Jackson about fifty miles, you turn west on Highway 84, a well-maintained parkway that runs all the way to Natchez, named for the Natchez Indians, an antebellum town perched on the banks of the Mississippi River, once a major landing for the steamers carrying cotton to the North and a large slave market. At one point, more millionaires lived in Natchez than in any other city in the country. In the sixties the Klan kept a storefront office on the main street.

The land consists of gently rolling hills covered with a thick forest of loblolly pine, tupelo, pin oak, maple, sycamore, and, by the rivers, cypress and sweet gum trees. Heading west, the country gains a certain magical feel; the trees grow up to the edge of the road, and narrow lanes curve off into darkness. There are few people to be seen. Occasionally, you come to an attractive, brick ranch-style house or a nicely kept trailer home with a garden alongside. There are no gas stations, hamburger stands, or furniture stores—not even an occasional bait stand.

In the national forest, which is easy to enter unawares, you soon wonder if you must keep track of how you got in so you can get out. You might expect eventually to come to a wide crossroads, where a few wooden shacks sit next to a dilapidated grocery store with a drooping porch, and battered pickups with gun racks and rebel flags in the rear windows are parked at random angles, and old men in straw hats with black bands and sweat stains under their arms listen to the radio and carve chunks of wood or play dominos, and a few dirty, near-naked kids scamper about in the dust, and a scrawny, three-legged yellow dog wanders aimlessly down the dirt road. Instead, you never leave an unspoiled land of great trees and deep rivers, a forest running free with fish and wildlife under brilliant blue skies. A primitive, fertile land that seems barely settled.

The four-lane parkway comes to the town of Meadville, the county seat and home in the sixties to one of the deadliest Klaverns of the Mississippi White Knights of the Ku Klux Klan, itself the deadliest Klan in the South. A land of unspeakable violence and matchless beauty. "Welcome to Meadville," the Lions sign says. As you descend the hill, you pass a hospital, a VFW club, and a cemetery, and eventually you come to the town square. In the middle sits the three-story brick courthouse, which has a handicapped ramp and free parking. Around the square are all the businesses you would expect to find in a vibrant small community: a clothing store, a public library, banks, a post office, the telephone company, lawyers' and CPAs' offices, and a little museum on the corner. On the edge of town are a family medical clinic and a convalescent home, with carefully mowed grass and rings of flowers. The streets are numbers one way and trees the other, like First and Elm or Second and Birch.

Meadville has few restaurants and no bars, but there are churches on almost every corner, most of them Baptist or Methodist. Meadville doesn't have black "quarters," like Bude and many other small Mississippi towns, although most of the town is either black or white. Continuing west out of town, you pass a discount food and tobacco market, and then you come to Della Mae's drive-in restaurant, which was an ice cream stand when Charles Moore and Henry Dee stood across the street hitchhiking on the morning of May 2, 1964. A large sign on the edge of town declares that the Franklin County Bulldogs were state high school football champions in 2006.

Charles Moore was known as Nub, and Henry Dee was teasingly called "Pimp" by some of his classmates because of his sharp clothes and easy manners. The two young men were headed toward the town of Roxie, thirteen miles west on Highway 84. Moore, who had recently been suspended from all-black Alcorn College for participating in a demonstration over conditions in the cafeteria, lived with his mother in Roxie, a hamlet where semi trucks parked side by side in the center of the one-block business district. Dee, not long back from Chicago, worked in a sawmill in town. If the white Volkswagen that picked them up had stayed headed west on 84, rather than turning off into the Homochitto National Forest, it would have passed what was known in the area as the Bunkley Community, home of the Bunkley Klavern.

Bunkley wasn't a town or village, but it was a community of sorts. The majority of the members of the Franklin

County Klavern lived on Bunkley Road. Clyde Seale, father to James, Jack, Don, and Gene, was the Exalted Cyclops of the Klavern. He owned a lot of land along Bunkley Road, which he farmed and logged. Archie Prather, who raised Charles Edwards, owned land there as well. On a piece of that land stood a building referred to as the Bunkley Rod and Gun Club. The Bunkley Klan met there every Saturday night. Further on up the road was the Bunkley Baptist Church, where most of the Klavern attended services. Bunkley, it is said, was a state of mind.

The Volkswagen, if it hadn't turned off 84, would eventually have come to Roxie. Dropped off there, Moore would have made his way home to see his mother, whom he knew was not feeling well, and Dee would have walked to the sawmill to pick up his check. The two friends might have met later that evening at the dance in Bude (as in "Jude"), across the road from Meadville.

Some of the roads in the area bear the names of the characters in this play. Seale Road leads deep into the wooded hills on the way to a small black cemetery, where Charles Moore is buried. The cemetery is enclosed by a barbed wire fence with longleaf pines and oaks on the edges. Charles lies only a few feet from the barbed wire, but in the shade of the tall trees. The handmade cement headstone, speckled white and splotched with moss, reads in rough letters,

Cherlie Eddie Moor
B. Aug. 10, 1944
Beried July 1964
Darling, we will miss you
Anywhere in Glory Is All Right

The grave, covered in a soft blanket of oak leaves, pine needles, and pinecones, has sunk at least a foot. A few graves nearby are decorated with plastic flowers.

Henry Dee is buried in a cemetery outside the small town of Kirby. Dee's mother was in a mental institution and was never told of her boy's death. His four sisters went on with their lives.

Jack Davis, who lives just east of Meadville, was by most accounts a member of the Bunkley Klavern. He denies it but does admit to being a member of Americans for the Preservation of the White Race (APWR), which was widely believed to be a front for the Klan. Davis was called to the stand in a pretrial hearing to support a motion by the defense to exclude a "confession" by Seale when Seale and Edwards were first arrested for the murders of Moore and Dee in the fall of 1964. Davis testified that not long after his release Seale showed him some bruised ribs and said he got them from the cops.

On the stand, Davis, like Seale and many of the other elderly witnesses, had to wear a black plastic hearing device in his ear. "Come back with that one. Come back please," he kept saying in response to questions from lead prosecutor Paige Fitzgerald. He was adamant and unrepentant about the APWR's good intentions in building a new school for whites only. When pressed on its racist nature, he shot back indignantly that they weren't telling anybody what to do. They were just trying to give whites a choice not to go to school with blacks.

The whites in Franklin County, it turned out, were too poor to build and run a private school for their children. Since 1969, when Mississippi finally complied with *Brown vs. Board of Education* under direct order of the U.S.

Supreme Court, the schools in Franklin County have been fully integrated. "If we'd a known then how easy it was gonna turn out, we wouldn't of gone crazy," one local said.

James Kenneth Greer, a former Klansman turned FBI informer now living in Natchez, has been following the trial. He understands the nature of the fear in those days. Whites grew up hearing at home and at school that blacks were inferior and lazy, that they stank and were sexually depraved. When the whites realized the North was attempting to integrate their schools, they felt it necessary to defend their children and themselves by any means necessary. "People in the South, especially people with young girls, they just couldn't stand the idea, and I was one of them, of putting their children in school with them nigger boys."

Doris Norman, a black woman living on the road coming into Roxie, not far from where Seale was living when he was arrested, believes that people learn to hate as children. A pastor at the New Hope Missionary Baptist Church in Natchez, she is not bitter, in spite of what she's lived through: crosses burned on lawns, churches burned to the ground, friends beaten for no reason. The hardest to understand was the white man himself: How could he have babies with a black woman and still hate her?

Justice was whatever the white man said it was. Years back, a few yards down the road from her home stood a store owned by a white man named George Ames. He built a house for a black woman and put her in it. She had a husband whose name was also George, and White George—that's what they started calling him—would beat Black George bloody whenever he came around his wife's new house. Then White George would have his way with Black George's wife, who was high yellow herself, never had children by either of the men, and thought herself superior. Finally, Black George had had enough: one day he got a gun and went inside the store and blew White George away. He had a trial, and everyone was saying he was a nigger, and he killed a white man, and he need to be hung from a tree, and the blacks believed it would happen. But then some whites said Black George took a lot from White George and that White George had it coming. So the whites let Black George go and told him to get out of the state. He left for Chicago and never did come back. Norman has wondered ever since what became of him.

CHAPTER 7

A scab has formed on Seale's forehead, and he picks at it gently as he watches the questioning. His scrawny shoulders jump when he chuckles at a remark whispered by one of his lawyers. He has one band of gray hair across the top of his head. Behind wire glasses his eyes are barely noticeable. He is not a well man: he has tumors on his kidneys, painful bone spurs, stints in both femoral arteries and emphysema. He's on painkillers and oxygen at the jail. It seems at any moment he could take a deep breath, fall forward onto the table and expire.

One prospective juror says he thinks *Mississippi Burning* was a good movie because it shows Mississippi in a positive light, as trying to clean up its past. Another juror, who saw *Mississippi Burning* and *Ghosts of Mississippi*, hates the way Mississippi is presented in both of them. *Mississippi Burning* is a black eye, and he hates coming from a state with all these old murders. When asked if he would hesitate to acquit because it might give the state one more black eye, he pauses, then says no. It feels like the only untruthful response of the day.

A black woman in the jury pool says she hasn't heard a single word about the Seale case. She has seen both movies and her opinion is that the crimes happened in the past and should stay in the past. Leave this one lay where it is. Another black woman confirms the notion that the basic cause of racial tension is that white people think they are superior to black people. Personally, she's never been discriminated against; maybe it's because her mother raised her to be a strong black woman, which she is.

A white woman is really pissed off about the whole thing: She's lost $800 in wages so far, and she can't afford to lose any more, not to mention a three-hour drive back and forth every day. After sitting around here for eleven hours, she sure as hell would hold it against the government. In her mind the unemployed and those on welfare should be the ones selected for juries. And yes, she feels she is discriminated against every day because she is white; she knows she's been passed over for jobs because of her race. A close member of her family belongs to the KKK, and other members have gone to meetings. This whole thing is a waste of time.

Among the prospective jurors, the women in particular seem fat; one after another, they heave their bulk up a step to the stand, often relying on the assistance of a marshal. The women also cry a lot. One woman, freaked out over her kids being without a mother for so long, cries three times on the stand before the judge finally excuses her.

Fitzgerald surfaces another worrisome bias. Why did it take the government so long to bring the case? What does it know now that it didn't know then? What about the others involved? One woman puts it this way: it seems to her it would take more than one guy to heave a man tied to an engine block over the side of the boat. A man points out that the case is being brought now because it's the "right time"; forty years ago Seale would never have been convicted. The problem is, the man says, memories fade with time; you tell stories and they become memories; repetition makes them the truth, and things are forgotten.

Fitzgerald has no good answer as to why the government waited this long to prosecute. There was a time long ago when charges could have been brought against all seven alleged participants: James, Daddy Clyde, brother Jack, Ernest Parker, Archie Prather, Curtis Dunn, and Charles Edwards, the rat. Thomas Moore, the black community, the state, the country, and history are going to have to settle for the prosecution of this one elderly man for the crimes that seven men committed against the two black teenagers. In truth, if it had been solely up to the authorities, this latest act in Mississippi's redemption drama would not now be on stage.

James Ford Seale and Charles Marcus Edwards were arrested on November 6, 1964, and charged with the murders of Charles Moore and Henry Dee. Edwards was arrested at 5:25 A.M., and by 9:07 that morning he had made a statement saying that he, Seale, and some "others" had picked up Dee and another unknown Negro male at Meadville with the intention of whipping them because his wife had spotted Dee "peeping" at her through the windows. The men took the two youths to the woods and whipped them, but the two were alive when he last saw them. Edwards didn't know what happened to them after that and refused to give other names.

Those facts alone suggested numerous state crimes: kidnapping, assault, assault with a deadly weapon, attempted murder, accessory before the fact. The law had Edwards's confession and Seale's statement to the cops that he had done it, but they were going to have to prove it. Deals could possibly have been made that would have brought in the others involved and the murders could have been fleshed out, the rest of the story told, rats turned for lesser sentences, and multiple convictions obtained. J. Edgar Hoover crowed in a memo to President Johnson that the arrests of Seale and Edwards had resulted from an "extensive FBI investigation" and served as an example of the FBI's close cooperation with local authorities "in bringing to justice individuals responsible for racial violence in Mississippi."

The two men posted $5,000 bond and were released the next day. District Attorney Lenox Forman announced that he would take the matter to a grand jury in January. Then reality must have set in: This was Mississippi. The invasion of white kids from the North to register blacks to vote—the Mississippi Freedom Project, or Freedom Summer—had just taken place; the state was ablaze in crosses and church fires, and blacks were being beaten, shot, and dumped in rivers. The Klan ruled the county and feared no one, including the law. The Klan was the law. The Klan even threatened to kill FBI agents. And the Seales, particularly Exalted Cyclops Clyde and his youngest son, James, were the worst of them; they held Franklin County, black and white, under what lawmen would call a virtual reign of terror.

Forman, an elected official, knew that when the all-white jury acquitted the defendants of murder, as it surely would, he would have to return to the community he lived in. The prosecutor declared on January 5, 1965, that he did not have "sufficient evidence" to take the case to a grand jury. On January 11, "in the interests of justice," the affidavits were dismissed. Seale and Edwards walked.

There was one critical piece of evidence that Forman didn't have: the statement of Ernest Gilbert. Gilbert, a leader in the White Knights, was young, tall, good-looking, and a powerful speaker. On September 14, 1964, Gilbert told an FBI agent that a couple of days after the murder, Jack Seale and Ernest Parker had told him a story about "putting a couple of niggers in the river." The two men said they were having trouble sleeping at nights thinking about what they had done. When Gilbert asked why they were telling him the story, they responded that in case something happened to them, they wanted a Klan officer to help them out. Gilbert had more conversations with Parker and Jack, Clyde, and James Ford Seale over the course of the summer, and they told him everything about what had happened to those two boys that day. Gilbert had a hard time handling one fact: both boys had been alive when they were pushed over the edge of the boat into the river. When Gilbert commented that that seemed rather inhumane, Jack Seale shrugged that he hadn't wanted to shoot them and get blood all over the boat.

We will never know whether Gilbert decided at that moment to turn informant or whether the accumulation of bloody facts over the course of the summer months made him realize that he could not live with the images now in his head. We do know that when he made his statement in September, he told the FBI what he knew, and the government brought back the divers, who found the rest of the bodies and the engine block and rails right where he said they would be, in front of Parker's Landing. And what he gave them was more than enough for the state to charge all seven men with kidnapping and murder.

The feds, however, didn't give Gilbert's statement to the Highway Patrol or the district attorney's office. It was well-known that the patrol and local sheriffs' offices were heavily infiltrated by the Klan: over half of the sheriff's department in Meridian belonged to the Klan, Neshoba County deputy Cecil Price belonged to the Klan, Franklin County Sheriff Wayne Hutto belonged to the Klan, Highway Patrolman Bernice Beasley, who worked Franklin County, was also a Klan member. Had the FBI given the statement to the local authorities, Gilbert would most likely have been killed within days, and other informants would have gone to ground. Besides, Gilbert was now a paid informant, and the bureau had further use of him. (Gilbert received $5,000 for his statement in the Seale case but later argued that he should have received twice that amount because his information led to the finding of two bodies.)

FBI Special Agent James Ingram was incensed by Forman's dismissal of the charges against Seale and Edwards; the district attorney could easily have prosecuted them with what he had. But the federal government also could have prosecuted. It could have protected Gilbert and done exactly what it did in 2006: immunize Edwards and turn him into a rat. If the federal government had looked at the case, it would have found adequate grounds for jurisdiction. But it turned the case over to the local authorities, and when they dropped it the federal government didn't pick it up. All of the government's resources were now focused on investigating the murder of the three civil rights workers.

CHAPTER 8

Emmett Till is present for this trial, as he was present
for the trials of De La Beckwith, Bowers, Killen, and the
other Mississippi Klansmen. His murder was a pivot in
the civil rights movement. Rosa Parks said it gave her the
courage to refuse to move to the back of the bus.

On the face of it, Emmett, "Bobo," wasn't anything special. He was a fourteen-year-old boy from Chicago visiting
his country cousins in Mississippi. He was a little over-
weight, had a lisp, and was somewhat of a clown who liked
to show off. Like Moore and Dee, Emmett Till wasn't
really agitating anything. But unlike the murders of Moore
and Dee, which were soon forgotten, Emmett Till's murder, for a variety of reasons, immortalized him. Like two of
the three civil rights workers, he came from a large city in
the North, which made him more newsworthy. Emmett's
mother insisted that her son's body be returned to Chicago
for burial and that his casket remain open for viewing so
that the world could see her boy's face. The rippled, almost
featureless flesh contrasted shockingly with the photo of
Emmett taken not long before—a hat tilted back on his
head, a teasing grin on his face. Congressman Charles

Diggs from Michigan attended the trial, further legitimizing it as a political event. Emmett's wolf whistle at an attractive, young white female added a lurid aspect to the story. Finally, the two men acquitted of the murder were guilty of the crime. A few months after the trial, both men confessed in a *Look* magazine article for $2,000 apiece.

News of the crime hit the black culture in Mississippi hard. The black newspapers out of Memphis and New Orleans and magazines like *Jet* gave the trial and acquittal front-page coverage. L. C. Dorsey's father went to the drugstore in Drew to buy a copy of *Look* magazine, which was risky itself, but it was sold out.

A few years after the crime, Dorsey, then in her midteens, almost came to violence herself over Emmett Till on the small plantation where her family sharecropped. She was chopping cotton with a sharp-edged hoe a few feet behind the owner, a man known for treating his sharecroppers well—he paid cash at the end of harvest rather than waiting until spring—when he began bragging about how if he had been with the men who took the Till boy from his home, the body would never have been found. He explained matter-of-factly that he would have cut open the boy's stomach and sliced his intestines to let the air out, so he would never have floated to the surface. He went on about it, right in front of her, as if the boy's murder meant nothing. Furious, Dorsey raised the hoe to bring it down on the man's heel, but another worker reached in and grabbed her arm.

Emmett Till might wonder why his murderers had gone unpunished all these years. Through the 1990s and early 2000s, when the other Klansmen were being prosecuted and thrown in jail, his case lay untouched, although some people involved in the incident were still alive: Carolyn Bryant, the woman he had supposedly whistled at, for one, as well as some of the black men thought to have taken part in his murder. Maybe he was too young or the case was too old, but little was done about it.

Sometimes it seems hard to remember—or imagine, for those not then alive—exactly what it was like in this country, in the South, in the fifties. Nowadays, the Klan can seem like a bunch of anachronistic clowns, Ross Barnett and George Wallace and Orville Faubus and Lester Maddox like silly demagogues. When you look back, though, the story has a certain inevitable feel to it. The stereotype was true: Mississippi culture back then was monolithic. In 1963, shortly before the worst began, James Silver, a professor at Ole Miss, wrote a book entitled *Mississippi: The Closed Society*, and as if to prove his very point, the state drove him from the university shortly after its publication. Silver wrote, "The only option Mississippians have is whether to make an inevitable transition peaceable or bloody." It wasn't really an option. Mississippi would never abandon its way of life without a fight, and a bloody one at that.

Before the sixties, in the Jim Crow era, things in Mississippi were relatively peaceful. Everyone got along because everyone knew his place. The Negro's place was below the white man's; more specifically, it was below the poor white man's. The white power structure—the bankers, lawyers, and politicians who had bonded during their days at Ole Miss—understood the necessity of this order and exploited the fears of poor whites to keep it in place. They held out the possibility that one day the Negro might no longer be on the bottom rung, that the poor white man himself might end up there. The Negro would want his jobs, his houses, his churches, and, ultimately, his women.

There were also "the others" determined to upset God's given order: the outside agitators, the northerners, the federal invaders, the Communists, the Jews, the entire spectrum of non-Christians. Mississippi was built openly and without reservation or ambiguity—some might even say with pride—on the principle of absolute white supremacy, on the rock bottom belief—not a political or philosophical position—that the black man was inferior to the white man, a belief that would be maintained and enforced either through slavery, as it had been in the past, or by segregation, as it was in the present. It was against the law to serve a black at a white lunch counter, or to teach black and white kids in the same classroom, or for blacks and whites to have sex.

The newspapers, particularly the *Clarion-Ledger* and the *Jackson Daily News*, both owned by the Hederman family, were vitriolically segregationist and editorialized in support of the Citizens Council. The *Jackson Daily News* predicted violence against the U.S. Supreme Court after *Brown v. Board of Education* when it declared, as a result of the decision, that "dark red stains of that [human] blood will be on the marble steps of the United States Supreme Court." Local television stations cut off the networks when shows on civil rights were aired.

In 1956 Mississippi created an agency called the Mississippi State Sovereignty Commission, whose task it was to enforce segregation and keep track of those who challenged it. The commission investigated subversive activities, which meant, in part, passing along the license plate numbers of civil rights workers to the Klan. The commission also made regular financial contributions to the Citizens Council, referred to by Greenville editor Hodding Carter Jr. as the "uptown Klan," a group based in Jackson but that spread to other states, whose slogan was "States Rights and Racial Integrity" and whose task it was to bring economic pressure to bear on whites to insure continued conformity with segregation. The council's membership lists in many cities were identical to those of the chamber of commerce.

Looking back, it seems odd how naively the Klan went about protecting the culture of white supremacy. The very things they feared the most they ensured happened soonest. Many blacks had been killed in Mississippi in the years before the Neshoba County murders, several of them never even identified, but the murder of three civil rights workers, two white and one black, brought the FBI and the national media swarming down on Mississippi. Mickey Schwerner could never have registered enough blacks to vote in Meridian and Philadelphia to initiate the changes his death did. It was the age of television. The Klan should have understood it, with the media play on James Meredith, Bull Connor, the bloody marches, and the sit-ins. The cameras loved the dogs and the billy clubs. All the publicity, though, seemed only to encourage the Klan; in the fall of 1966, after Bowers had been charged with conspiracy in the murder of the three civil rights workers, he ordered the assassination of Vernon Dahmer in Hattiesburg.

The FBI thoroughly penetrated the Mississippi Klan in the sixties. Not long after Moore and Dee were murdered, Charles Edwards, Clyde Seale, and Archie Prather gathered around a bonfire and, on Imperial Wizard Bowers's orders, tossed their robes and Klan files into the flames.

Chapter 9

Shirley Seale, a distant relative of James Ford Seale and a pastor at a black church in Natchez, watches Seale's trial with interest and sadness. Her granddaddy, a leading member of the Klan in Natchez, taught her all about how lazy and corrupt niggers were, and he quoted scripture to prove it. As a little girl, she had watched him walk down Seale Road to an open pasture where men in robes and hoods stood in a circle around white crosses blazing against the night sky. As she grew older, he proudly took her along to the rallies. She became meaner than he was: she wouldn't let a black worker sit at the kitchen table to eat his noonday meal. She passed her attitudes along to her children, telling them she would disown them for either one of two things: being gay or marrying a nigger.

Shirley met her second husband, Gary, at a bar in Natchez. Gary had grown up in Roxie and attended segregated schools, where the inferiority of the black race was taught as fact. Students were encouraged to recite examples of this fact in class. He was twelve when the school integrated, and being around blacks made him so uncomfortable that he took himself out of school and never went back.

One Sunday, when his family was out on a drive in the Roxie countryside, they passed a burned-out car on the side of the road. His father pulled over for a look: inside the still-smoldering vehicle sat the charred body of a black man. Gary read in the paper that the law called the incident an accident, but that was impossible because the man was sitting in the backseat and there were three empty cans of gasoline in the trunk.

One of the first things Gary and Shirley asked each other that night in the bar was whether the other had ever been with a nigger. After both swore they hadn't and never would, the conversation went on. A few years after they got married, Gary went to a revival and came out of it a different man. He attended Bible school at the black New Hope Missionary Baptist Church and soon was sneaking over there for Sunday services. Shirley thought he was crazy, but eventually went along, just to shut him up. Meeting Bishop Stanley Searcy at the service, she threw her arms around him and pronounced him her brother. It was the first time she had touched a black man.

Shirley was ordained in the New Hope Church in 2005. Gary serves as a deacon. These days, she would rather see her daughter with a black man than some of the crack-smoking white trash running around Natchez and Franklin County. Many members of her family have disowned her and her husband. Her daughter has been warned that their house will be set on fire as the family sleeps in their beds.

Shirley's relative, the elderly man at the counsel table, the tattoo of a hula dancer on his left forearm covered by a long-sleeved dress shirt, appears to watch the proceedings with passive interest. The acts of which he is accused seem almost too powerful for him. Evil or innocence, you think, should have a face, but the aging countenance frustratingly reveals nothing. You wonder how the crime settled in his brain, in his heart, as time passed and the world and Mississippi moved on—whether he could maintain the violent fervor every time he thought about the murders over the years, or whether the crime and the passion had faded, and he saw the killings now as merely unpleasant chores.

Seale is here today only because he talked. If he had never breathed a word of what happened on May 2, he would never have felt the cold bite of shackles around his ankles. But it must have been too much for him; he had to put the memory, the images, to words and get them out of his head.

One wonders what distinguishes Seale from the white man who believed in separation of the races, or maybe even hated black people, but would never have resorted to violence. L. C. Dorsey, who grew up on a plantation in the Delta, believes there is a Seale in every community and that it's the weaker kid who ends up the killer. If a boy hears every day that blacks are violent, sexual animals and suffers some trauma himself, maybe witnesses a lynching or is bullied or picked on himself, it can turn that hate into violence. The feelings of weakness and trauma evolve into a violent rage toward people weaker than he.

The FBI reports indicate that Seale was obsessed with white people who associated with or employed blacks, particularly white men who went with black women. Seale and his friends would take them from their homes, strip them of their clothes, put them in the middle of a circle, and

whip them. In the end, you wonder if the killing violence
came from his dad: if his father taught him how to drive a
pickup and hunt and fish, maybe he also taught him how
to murder.

The passage of time must have given Seale comfort.
Thirty-five years and not a rustle from the feds or the
state. His eyes must have shot open one day at the breakfast table when he read that the state was reinvestigating
the Medgar Evers case. Then Bowers, the big dog, was indicted and convicted of killing Vernon Dahmer. Avants
went down for killing Ben Chester White. Seale must
have felt a little panic when in 2000 *Clarion-Ledger* reporter Jerry Mitchell appeared on his doorstep. "You ain't
got anything now that you didn't have back then," he told
Mitchell. "And that's nothing." He was right at that point:
although Mitchell had the Gilbert statement, Gilbert said
he would never testify, and Edwards, still adhering to the
Klan code of silence, was not yet a rat. Still, Seale must
have felt uneasy when strangers came around knocking on
his door after so many years. He must have felt uneasy
when Killen was convicted in 2005 of a crime that occurred only a few weeks after Dee and Moore were murdered. If he did, it didn't show; his last words to Mitchell
were, "Have at me."

Mitchell, a native Texan with a fondness for ice-cream-
colored shirts, has himself played a critical role in the prosecution of Klan murders in Mississippi and throughout
the South. He first developed information showing that
the Sovereignty Commission had sabotaged De La Beckwith's first trial for the Evers murder by feeding informa-

tion about the jurors to the prosecution. His series of articles created sufficient outcry for the district attorney to reopen the case.

Then, while investigating the murder of NAACP activist Vernon Dahmer, Mitchell developed an informant who said he had overheard a conversation in which Bowers gave the order to kill Dahmer. Bowers was charged, tried, and convicted of murder in 1998.

Bowers later gloated to Mitchell that he didn't particularly mind being in prison since the person responsible for the Neshoba killings was still a free man, referring, everyone thought, to Edgar Ray Killen. When Mitchell repeated the remark in print, it revived interest in Killen's case. Mitchell also reported that Killen, after his conviction, had been seen pumping gas, which resulted in the revocation of his appeal bond and his incarceration.

Finally, Mitchell destroyed the alibi of Bobby Frank Cherry, one of the suspects in the Birmingham church bombing that killed the four little girls. Cherry was subsequently tried and convicted of the crime in 2002.

CHAPTER 10

Jury selection continues. While the room waits for the judge to enter, Seale picks a scab from his forehead, looks at it, and flicks it onto the floor. Only a few feet away, Fitzgerald is conferring with defense lawyer Kathy Nester, and they share a laugh. The air in the courtroom doesn't reek of vengeance, as it does in cases where the murder is fresh and friends and families ache to see the perpetrator suffer. Henry Dee and Charles Moore have been dead too long; adjustments have been made to the reality of their murders, although Thomas Moore says all his life he's had nightmares about the two boys being beaten while tied to a tree. He still wonders if in the end his brother called out for him.

The inordinate amount of violence in the lives of the jurors is striking. One man tells a story about watching his nephew being beaten to death by a dump truck driver; another man's sister was beaten to death by her husband; one woman was sexually abused by her father, a member of the Klan, until she was eighteen years old; a female basketball coach had a friend who was shot and killed; another woman was subjected to ongoing abuse by her husband, who had disowned his stepdaughter because she had a baby by a black man; one woman had a brother who murdered his wife, then committed suicide; one man's niece had died in an assault. And so on.

A white businesswoman, well dressed and classy but very brittle, explains that she belongs to an organization called Transformation Jackson, a group of citizens who believe the road to redemption is through prayer for justice and righteousness. The group has specific prayer targets, and she and others went to the Killen trial in Neshoba County to pray. They have prayed for justice and righteousness to prevail at this trial as well. She believes that the redemptive power of God will bring Mississippi from the tail to the head (of what she doesn't say), from the bottom to the top, where it should be. "Isn't it just like God to do something like that?" she asks, lit up with a proud smile.

Juror 59 was growing up in Philadelphia, Mississippi (Neshoba County), when the three civil rights workers were murdered. He knows *Mississippi Burning* to be grossly inaccurate. The mayor, shown as a racist who committed suicide, in fact died of old age. And there weren't blocks and blocks of burning houses either, just one church. However, there was a lot of Klan activity in Philadelphia in those days. As a child, he watched Klansmen walk around in sheets during halftime at high school football games. He believed in it all back then, as well as that the federal government had no business telling Mississippi what to do. Although he now sees segregation as ridiculous, he still doesn't believe in mixing the races—marriage is hard enough without having kids who don't belong in either the black or white world.

Racial attitudes when this prospective juror was growing up weren't just about race—they were about living. Consider the two nineteen-year-olds who stood across the street from the ice cream stand on the west side of Meadville and stuck out their thumbs, a not uncommon practice in those days. When a white Volkswagen slowed down and the driver called out to ask the two if they wanted a ride, both boys hesitated and shook their heads. They were wary of the man behind the wheel. The White Knights had only been organized in Franklin County five months earlier, but they had already been active, and the black community talked among themselves about who was in the Klan.

Dorsey recalls that in those days blacks were socialized at an early age to an intricate set of rules and protocols: you avoided conflict with whites at all costs; you did whatever a white person told you to do; you never talked back to a white; if a white person touched you, you moved away and said you were sorry; you addressed a white person with yes sir, no ma'am; you were never alone around a white person of the opposite sex. You did nothing to frighten whites.

Dealing with whites could be a dangerous game; if you broke the rules, you might pay with your life. Dorsey was eleven years old when she heard on the radio that Emmett Till had been taken from his home outside Money and murdered. *Taken from his home.* Not even your parents could keep you safe; that was the scariest part. The white man had his foot on your neck, and if you squirmed, he would only push down harder, so you went along.

Jewell McDonald, whose mother and brother were two of the people pulled from their cars and beaten outside the Mount Zion Methodist Church in Philadelphia the night the church was burned (which eventually brought the three civil rights workers to town to investigate), remembers that Sheriff Lawrence Rainey and Deputy Cecil Price resented black men with facial hair; when they encountered one, they would cut the hair off with a knife or pull it out with pliers. Rainey kept a large cage in the back of a pickup at the station, and when he or Price arrested a black or an Indian (Choctaw), he put the person in the cage and slowly paraded him around town, stopping here and there, for all to see. One day, McDonald was almost put in the cage herself for a $20 overdraft on a bank, until a white friend came to her rescue.

Blacks in Neshoba County had their own community center where they often held dances on the weekend. When Sheriff Rainey and Deputy Price strode onto the floor wearing their Stetson hats and cowboy boots, guns on one hip, batons on the other, the music stopped abruptly. A space of three feet opened in front and on either side as they walked slowly through the crowd. "Y'all be out of town by eleven o'clock!" they called out. The music started back up the moment they left.

The rules could change from town to town. Burl Jones, the black man whom the Franklin County sheriff turned over to the Klan, remembers Fayette as one of the most dangerous communities in Southwest Mississippi. You could wear a white shirt in town only on Sunday, and if a white person approached you on the sidewalk, you stepped off into the street. You never looked a white man in the eye, and you never passed him on the highway. You were free to go into a white-owned store and buy clothes—as long as you didn't expect to try them on first.

Alex Alston, a semiretired, white, seventy-five-year-old Jackson trial lawyer who is observing much of the trial from the spectator seats, grew up the son of a motel owner in a small Delta town in the fifties. The caste system was something he took for granted: the lowest white man was higher than the highest black man. The rules were inviolable: a black man addressed you, even when you were a boy, as Mister Alex; you didn't shake a black person's hand (that alone was enough to make you a nigger lover); you always called blacks "niggers"; blacks always came to the back door of the house; blacks did not use parks or public facilities; a black man did not speak to a white woman; blacks were off the street when the curfew bell rang in the Chinaman's store at 11 P.M.

Despite all this, blacks were supposedly content and happy. If a white mistress asked her black cook if she liked her situation, she would reply, "Oh, yes, Ms. Jones, I loves you, Ms. Jones. I loves you." Whites, the ones he knew, loved blacks and would do anything for them, as long as they kept their place. Growing up in that small Delta town, Alston didn't see anything wrong with the way things were.

And that's how it was for Charles Moore and Henry Dee on the morning of May 2, 1964. Something warned them not to get into the Volkswagen with the young white man at the wheel, but when he pulled to a stop and ordered them to get in, they did as they were told.

Chapter 11

Seale is not charged with murder. He is charged with three violations of federal law: conspiracy to kidnap, kidnapping Henry Dee, and kidnapping Charles Moore. Murder, in and of itself, is not a federal crime unless it occurs on federal property. Kidnapping is not a federal crime either, unless you transport the victim alive across state lines. Murder is a state crime, in and of itself, as is kidnapping.

Neither the state nor the federal government showed any interest in investigating the murders of Dee and Moore from January 1965 until 1998. To a large extent, this trial is happening because of Connie Chung and her documentary film producer, Harry Phillips, from ABC's *20/20*. Looking to do a story on unsolved civil rights murders in Mississippi, after De La Beckwith was put away, Chung and Phillips took a look at the Ben Chester White murder. The three men involved in that crime had all walked: Jack Jones, who watched the killing, was never charged; Claude Fuller, who pumped over ten bullets into White, was let go after his trial resulted in a hung jury; and Ernest Avants, who confessed twice to lawmen to shooting White's head off with a shotgun, was acquitted in state court. The case was so unnoteworthy that local law enforcement hadn't even kept track of the investigative files or the trial transcripts. After all, double jeopardy prevented a second shot.

Fortunately for Mississippi, and unfortunately for Avants, Chung and Phillips weren't so easily dismissed. In the musty basement of the Natchez Historical Society, Phillips found boxes and boxes of old cases. Among them was the transcript of the Avants trial. These two nonlawyers quickly found a basis for federal jurisdiction: White was murdered in the Homochitto National Forest. A young fisherman found his body lying in a riverbed below a road running through the heart of the forest. There was no evidence indicating he had been murdered somewhere else. U.S. Attorney Brad Pigott and his predecessors, as well as the FBI and the local press, don't seemed to have looked at the case and missed this fact; they apparently hadn't looked at the case at all. By this point, of course, the last man standing was Avants, sixty-nine years old. The killers had lived out their lives, while the means and method to take their freedom from them were in "plain sight."

Chung and Phillips kept their mouths shut about their discovery until they arranged for an interview with Ernest Avants at his trailer in the town of Bogue Chitto. You can tell from Avants's cocky attitude that he is not worried—he has been acquitted after all—and he makes little pretense of being a reformed racist. He is Mississippi's worst nightmare: the unreconstructed redneck braggart Klansman, and proud of it. Leaning on his elbows, facing Chung, the craggy white-haired man talks about the way it was:

AVANTS: A white man has run this world. A white man has run this United States. That's why it's great like it is. . . . The Jews own Adams County, and the Catholics run it, and the niggers enjoy it. [Chuckle.]

When Chung asks him if he killed White, Avants flat-out denies it. When Chung reads to him Jones's statement in which he says Avants blew White's brains out, Avants says he never heard that read. He asks, Why, if this nigger was killed the way they say he was, why wouldn't the buzzards eat him? The buzzards won't eat nothing that dies of rabies or poison.

CHUNG: Back then, white people probably would not convict a white person for killing a black man.
AVANTS: Like they would now.

ABC aired the show, and Chung and Phillips took their "discovery" that White was killed in the national forest to U.S. Attorney Brad Pigott, who got Avants indicted for one count of murder. Paige Fitzgerald parachuted in from Washington, D.C., and, along with Jack Lacy from the U.S. Attorney's Office, prosecuted and convicted Ernest Avants, who went to jail for life. Something that could have been tried in 1966, when all three killers were alive.

ABC News filmed the arrest. As Avants is being led from the trailer in cuffs, Chung calls out questions to him. An elderly woman inside the trailer hollers, "Get her out of here, or I'm going to blow her brains out." Just what Mississippi needed to enhance its image: a trash-talking white woman threatening to blow the brains out of a celebrity newswoman.

Chung and Phillips weren't done. Looking for another case, they came across the murders of Henry Dee and

Charles Moore. Phillips asked Pigott for the case files, and according to one source in the U.S. Attorney's Office, Pigott agreed to turn them over to Phillips in exchange for outtakes—unshown footage—of the ABC interview with Avants, which might contain damaging admissions by the defendant. Phillips adamantly denies the arrangement, but one way or another, he got the files, which contained the unredacted statement of informer Ernest Gilbert as he gave it to the FBI in September 1964.

FBI agents promise informants that their names will never be revealed and that they will never be called to testify. Otherwise, the bureau would never get any informants. Pigott reportedly said he thought Gilbert was dead; the odds are, anxious to nail Avants, he didn't give the Dee-Moore file much thought when he turned it over. He certainly didn't give it enough consideration in 2000 to seriously consider prosecuting Seale, cutting short his freedom by seven years. With Gilbert alive to affirm his statement, he might not have needed a rat, and Edwards could have found himself in Fitzgerald's sights along with Seale, rather than being her chief witness.

Chung and Phillips found Ernest Gilbert and his wife in a small town in Louisiana. Gilbert had informed for the FBI into the mid-seventies, earning over $30,000. He lived in constant fear; the Seales, perhaps suspicious after the remains of Moore and Dee were found in the river where they had told him they were located, had threatened his life several times. Finally, it got a little too hot, and he quit the FBI and the Klan altogether.

Phillips approached the old Klansman and explained that Chung wanted to interview him. Gilbert was angry that the government had revealed his identity. After getting advice from the local chief of police, a black man, Gilbert finally agreed to the interview. Phillips went to Gilbert's home several times, but he never knew what sort of reception he was going to receive: on one visit, Gilbert threatened to shoot him if he came any further on his land; another time, he greeted him quite warmly and invited him inside. During the interviews Gilbert smoked constantly—every so often his wife would replace the full ashtray on the table with a clean one—and often he would almost collapse in fits of guilt and remorse. In the end, Phillips got what he needed.

That episode of *20/20* began with the man who would become the central figure in this drama. The camera shows Chung and Phillips approaching Seale's RV in Roxie. Once Seale realizes who is at his door, he calls out, "The best thing for you is to get your ass up that hill." When Phillips asks him if he had anything to do with the killing, Seale repeats, "Get on up the hill." Which Phillips does, perhaps familiar with Seale's reputation for gunplay.

In the next scene, the camera finds Edwards sitting at a table. Stocky, ruddy-faced, left eye a little askew, he seems a pleasant-enough fellow. Asked by Chung, who has his 1964 statement, if he had anything to do with the murder, he flat-out denies it; the FBI agents are lying when they say he made that statement. When Chung asks him if he has anything against blacks, he replies with a nervous smile that back then he guesses he was prejudiced.

Then Chung turns to Gilbert. Archival clips show a tall figure speaking passionately at Klan rallies, declaring that the white people in Mississippi are going to war and to hell with those who try to stop them. If it were up to him, he would shoot "every damn nigger" who demonstrated or burned a building. Now, at seventy-five, Gilbert's black hair has turned gray, but he is still an imposing figure, and he speaks directly to the camera as he explains that back then he was the Imperial Wizard of the White Knights of the KKK and that he recruited police and sheriff deputies to the organization. His eyes are deep and haunted, and his voice seems to stagger as he wanders through his violent past.

GILBERT: Those kids were abused awful and beaten—and they begged for their lives. I was told all of this. And then they were taken to the Mississippi River, weights were tied on them, and they were thrown in the river alive.

CHUNG: Alive?

GILBERT: Alive.

CHUNG: How did you react to that?

GILBERT: Like I said, I lost my mind. I lost my soul. And I finally decided something had to be done.

GILBERT: God told Cain, your brother's blood cries out to me from the ground . . . I want—I want—I want justice for those kids, that's what I want.

CHUNG: That's why you've come forward now?

GILBERT: Yes. This is not about me; this is not about you. This is about two little kids who were brutally murdered. And were innocent.

Even thirty-six years after the murder, Gilbert doesn't want justice for the two boys badly enough to testify against their killers. He says, "Hell no," to the idea. "They have all the information. What good is it going to do me to get up there and testify—and people say, well hell, he was one of them. How can he testify again? Any juror is going to turn them loose."

This segment of *20/20* closes with Edwards almost gloating about the good life he's had. "It's been good. I've raised—I've had a good job all my life, and I raised five kids, had the American dream."

The team of Chung and Phillips had done it again. They'd blown open their second Klan murder case from the sixties. Now, as in the Avants case, it was up to the authorities to prosecute those still alive. Except nothing happened. In the face of Gilbert's refusal to testify, the government figured they were stumped. One might think that if Phillips could convince Gilbert to sit and tell his story on camera, the federal government, with all its resources, including the formidable skills of former FBI agent Jim Ingram and the threat of a subpoena, should have been able to get him to tell the truth to a grand jury. Then there would have been two defendants in the murder of Henry Dee and Charles Moore.

The government promised to take another look at the case, but nothing came of it. Apparently it didn't occur to the U.S. attorney to immunize Edwards and take a run at Seale.

CHAPTER 12

The play on stage on the third floor of the federal court-house continues. Now the prospective jurors must be in-troduced to the alleged facts of the case. The calm but imposing black judge, sitting like Moses on a throne, moves to the next scene by reading aloud in his smooth baritone the specifics of Seale's alleged crimes. The slow, deliberate pacing of his recitation of the gruesome facts gives the story a particularly horrorlike quality; he abbreviates "White Knights of the Ku Klux Klan" to W-K-K-K-K, and the way he rolls it off, like the slow motion firing of a ma-chine gun, makes James Seale seem even more menacing. The prospective jurors sit spellbound.

This is exactly what defense attorney Kathy Nester is scared of: Seale is going to be tried for being a member of the Klan. Since the crimes supposedly involved a Klan conspiracy, the prosecutor will bring in evidence of the Klan's "reign of terror," and her client will be found guilty by association. Make him scary enough, and the jury will convict him for that alone. She has objected continuously to this evidence in pretrial motions—and consistently gone down in flames.

The judge's recitation of the alleged facts leaves some prospective jurors visibly shaken. He proceeds to tell them how, in considering the defendant's guilt or innocence, they must leave their feelings and biases aside. One white woman on the panel challenges him on what he means by feelings and biases and wonders how you set them aside. She has two young boys, and when she saw Seale's picture on TV, she asked herself how he could do that to those boys. Does that mean she's biased? Although she believes him guilty now, she'll try to put that belief aside, but she's not sure she'll be able to. And how can she know now whether she'll be able set her beliefs aside when she gets to the jury room? She has other feelings here: he's guilty until proven innocent. Would she want someone like her on her jury? she is asked. Oh, no, she says. The judge pressures her a little: Couldn't she leave all that behind? She'd try, but in the end, no, she really would want to hear something from the defendant. She would want to see him on the stand.

The woman is saying what is in everyone's mind: if you don't get up, deny your guilt, and tell your side of the story, you must have something to hide. Seale can't take the stand; he's denied that he was ever in the Klan, and that denial would allow Fitzgerald to smother the jury with even more evidence of his participation in "the reign of terror." She would do her best to provoke an outburst, so the jury could see—could feel—the racial resentment still percolating in his soul.

In this drama, even the defense must renounce the past. Nester and her co-counsel can't get up and say, hey, that's the way it was back then—half the white people in Franklin

County were in the Klan, the other half were sympathetic, and everyone said "nigger" in everyday conversation. She can't go, "Those were the days when. . . ." Every Mississippian has experienced too much shame and guilt and anger over the years, and no one wants to hear it. The facts, the judge keeps saying; you have to try him on the facts. But emotions themselves are facts, and like the lady said, who knows what you can do about your emotions when it's closing time?

The observers on the right side of the room, behind the prosecution table, have no doubt about Seale's guilt. They've read about the 1964 statements of Ernest Gilbert, Charles Edwards, and Seale, and long before any facts have been presented in a court of law, some articles in the press have recited the alleged facts of the case almost as if they were already established.

The prosecution had wanted badly to get Gilbert's 1964 statement into evidence. Coupled with Edwards's 2006 statement, it would pin Seale to the wall like a butterfly. In damning detail, Gilbert repeated to the agents what Seale and the others had told him. When the boys got in the car, Seale said he was a revenue agent and asked if they knew of any illegal stills in the area. On the ride one of the boys asked to get out. Seale refused and said he wanted them to meet some other agents.

Clyde Seale, Charles Edwards, and Curtis Dunn were following behind the car in a pickup truck, and after Seale alerted them on a walkie-talkie, both vehicles rolled deep into the national forest. When the Volkswagen eventually pulled over, the pickup came to an abrupt stop behind it. Seale ordered the boys out. He grabbed his rifle and "got the drop on the two Negroes." The Klansmen tied the boys to trees and beat them with "bean poles," while Clyde interrogated them about guns in the black community and the "Negro trouble in Franklin County." The beating continued until one of the boys said that the guns were stored in Preacher Briggs's church in Roxie.

Jack Seale told Gilbert that he'd received a call that morning from his father in which Clyde had repeated the letters "K-I-W-U," which stood for "Klansman, I want you." Sometime later, Jack Seale and Ernest Parker showed up at Clyde's farm in Parker's red Ford. The boys had been beaten bloody. The men laid a piece of plastic tarpaulin in the trunk of the Ford to prevent bloodstains, and Dee and Moore were stuffed inside. They drove the car to the Ole River near Tallulah, Louisiana. When they got there, Parker and Jack Seale were surprised to find the boys still alive. The men chained them to an engine block, took them out into the river in a boat and tossed them over the side alive.

Gilbert said that Parker told him he was worried that the serial numbers on the engine block could be traced back to him. And he worried that his brother, Robert, who knew nothing of the incident and occasionally dipped a cup in the water as he boated across the river, might accidentally drink water off a dead Negro.

U.S. Attorney Dunn Lampton knew the problem with the statement: it was double and triple hearsay—what Seale told Gilbert, who told the agent, who wrote it in a document. It wasn't even Gilbert's out-of-court statement; it was what the agent said his out-of-court statement was. But Lampton wasn't sure he had a winnable case without it.

Lampton was a homegrown Mississippi prosecutor, having been elected district attorney of the Fourteenth Judicial District (made up of three counties) seven times. An excellent trial lawyer, he once tried and won three murder cases in one week. George W. Bush had appointed him U.S. attorney one day before September 11, and he immediately became immersed in national-security issues. He had watched with interest, however, as Assistant U.S. Attorney Jack Lacy and Special Litigation Counsel for the Department of Justice Paige Fitzgerald brought Ernest Avants to the federal dock and slammed him in jail for life for the 1966 murder of Ben Chester White.

Prior to the Killen trial, Canadian filmmaker David Ridgen had contacted Donna Ladd, editor of the *Jackson Free Press*, to discuss other possible cold civil rights cases in Mississippi. Both were interested in the Dee-Moore case, and they decided to work together on resurrecting it. They decided that Ridgen would contact Thomas Moore in Colorado Springs and try to convince him to come back to Mississippi to search for justice in the killing of his brother and Henry Dee. They would meet Ladd and her photographer in Franklin County right after the Killen trial and cover Moore's journey together. During the July 2005 visit, Moore quickly learned that Seale was still alive and called Lampton to talk about his brother's murder.

Lampton read the case file the night before the meeting and was stunned that nothing had been done about the crime for forty-one years. At the meeting, Moore and Lampton discovered that they had served in the same unit in the 1991 Gulf War—Moore as a command sergeant major and Lampton as a colonel judge advocate general.

Lampton promised Moore he would take a serious look at the case, but privately he had doubts. Edwards's 1964 statement about him and Seale beating the boys in the woods couldn't be authenticated. Seale's alleged confession—"Yes, I did it, but I'm not going to admit it. You're going to have to prove it"—could easily be seen more as a boast or a challenge. The crime occurred in a national forest, true, but the statute of limitations on kidnapping was six years. The Lindberg Law, under which they would have to proceed, required proof that the victim had been kidnapped and taken across state lines alive—proof Lampton didn't have without Gilbert's statement. Others in his office had previously looked at the case and concluded that nothing could be done. The district attorney in Natchez had also declined to prosecute the murders, which appeared to have occurred in his jurisdiction.

Lampton needed to turn either Seale or Edwards. He believed that Edwards, the weaker of the two, knew what had happened after the whipping in the forest, whether he was there or not. They needed to loosen his tongue. An attorney in Lampton's office suggested a way to force him to talk: Immunize him. Tell him he'll go to jail if he doesn't cooperate. You let one walk to get one. One out of seven, but better than none out of seven.

CHAPTER 13

Thomas Moore is treated as a venerated figure in the courtroom. He sits quietly in the front row, next to his son. Those in the rows behind cast glances in his direction as the worst facts come out. At the end of the day, reporters corner him outside on the steps of the courthouse, and he usually obliges with a good quote or two ("We are on the doorstep of justice," he says one day). Moore has had a good life, by his own account. He kept his promise to his mother and didn't look back. He married his Roxie sweetheart and stayed in the army for thirty years (and fifteen days, as he always says), retiring in 1994, after rising to the highest enlisted rank and serving in Vietnam, Panama, Korea, and the Gulf War. Along the way, he obtained bachelor's degrees in social work and sociology.

Thomas got a long way out of Mississippi—but never all the way. You can see the determination on his heavy brow, the tension in the set of his jaw, and the suffering in the deep hollows of his eyes. In 1964 he had been drafted into the army, going through basic training at Fort Polk, Louisiana, when his brother and Henry Dee went missing. He didn't learn about it until he came home on leave in

June. When he left a few weeks later, the two were still missing. In mid-July, he was playing ping-pong on the base when his commanding officer called him into his office to tell him the partial remains of his brother had been found in the Mississippi River.

Moore arrived home in Roxie to complete silence. No one talked about what had happened. No one. Not the minister at the funeral service. Not his mother. Not his aunts and cousins. Friends. It was almost as if his brother had never really been. Thomas had identified the brass buckle found on his brother's belt; it bore an *M*, for Moore. Thomas himself had given it to him for his birthday.

The boys' father had died when they were little, and their mother had worked hard to keep food on the table in their small house outside Roxie, which had neither running water nor electricity. She had been very protective of the boys—now don't you go messing around with them white women, she would say, knowing the one thing that would get them killed. The brothers didn't know about civil rights protests or marches, but they knew how life was in Southwest Mississippi.

Thomas and Charles walked and hitchhiked every day; it was how they got places. The boys had developed a plan: if a car picked them up, one boy would sit in back, one in front; if there was trouble, the one in back would grab the driver by the neck and the one in front would hit the brake. If they were in a truck, the boys would wait until they crossed a bridge and jump out into the water. But there had never been trouble before.

Thomas has a hard time with one particular thing about what happened to his brother and Henry Dee: Seale could have interrupted the death ride any time he wanted; he could have let the boys out of the car at the turn into the forest; he could have let them go after the beating; he could have stopped the crime at the farm, before loading the boys into the trunk; he could have halted it on the riverbank itself, or even on the boat. He could have looked at Charles and Henry, seen human beings, and had second thoughts; he could have said, Jesus, what are we doing here, killing these boys? At least he could have shot them before putting them in the boat. But he didn't.

After the murders, Thomas often found his mother sitting in the kitchen crying. "I just wish he would come through that doorway," was all she ever said. There was nothing she or anyone else could do about it; only trouble would come from trying. A newspaper reported that she had repeatedly praised the citizens of Franklin County, undoubtedly to ensure that no further harm came to her family. She died twelve years after the murders at sixty-five. Thomas wishes he had talked to her more about his brother's death.

It wasn't uncommon for the Klan in those days to pick up a black man for one sin or another and release him unharmed, or harmed but not dead. Burl Jones, sitting in the courtroom, figures he was a whole lot luckier than Charles Moore and Henry Dee. He could well have ended up in the river, just like they did. That same summer of 1964, he had gotten on the wrong side of Highway Patrolman Beasley (there are varying versions as to how), a known Klansman, and the last time he was arrested, Beasley stuck him in the Meadville jail, where he stayed for three days.

On his release, he ran straight into a setup: waiting at the bottom of the stairs were two hooded men gripping base-ball bats. They whacked him on the head, then marched him outside, pulled a cloth over his head, and shoved him into the trunk of a car. They drove into the night, eventu-ally pulling over on an isolated country road. The men got him out, dragged him through the woods and tied him with thick ropes to a tree. After cutting his pants and shirt away, they began lashing him with bullwhips, all the while questioning him about guns in the area, about Preacher Briggs at the First Baptist Church in Roxie, and about a black man working on the electrical lines. Jones repeatedly denied knowing anything about any of it. He became con-vinced that he was going to die and prayed for it to be quick. One of the men suggested they take him and dump him somewhere; the other insisted they kill him on the spot. The two argued heatedly back and forth, until finally they offered him a deal: they would spare his life in return for him getting out of town and never coming back. His captors dumped him alongside the ditch a few miles down the road, where he lay until a black family found him, the side of his head caved in, most of the skin torn off his back, and took him home.

The next day Jones managed to pack a suitcase and get on a bus to Chicago, where he worked as a deputy sheriff for the next thirty years. Sitting here in the courtroom, he thinks back on that day and feels proud, as he has over the years, that he never begged the men for his life. He lives in Natchez now, and the city—all of Mississippi, in fact—seems like a different country. He feels more comfortable around white people down here now than he did up north.

His white neighbor even mows his lawn when he's out of town. The white waitress in the diner where he goes for coffee hugs him when he comes in, something that would have got him hanged forty-five years ago. He felt a little sorry for Seale, as old and sick as he is, until he saw him smiling and joking with his family. Seale cheated those boys of their lives, of the possibility of experiencing the finer things in life, like beautiful women and good whiskey. Jones's own chance for justice is long past, but he's happy it's finally here for these boys.

Although it's late May, the famous Mississippi heat has yet to arrive. The air is light and brisk, and occasionally it lifts the state flag in front of the governor's mansion across the street from the courthouse, laying out the white stars in the blue crossed bars on a blaze of red. Watching the parade of characters walk down the steps of the court-house, camera crews waiting to pounce, you wonder if the view of those days is, and always will be, too dense and corrupt, too obstructed by shame and paradox, to ever be fully illuminated. People who tried to live otherwise honest, God-fearing lives, who loved their children and cared well for their parents in old age, managed for centuries to treat a race of people as little more than beasts of burden.

Henry Dee's four sisters walk down the street arm in arm. Thelma Collins does all the talking to a reporter, who keeps bumping into his cameraman as he walks backward. Jack Davis, by accounts a template for white supremacy and violence in his youth, now almost deaf, toddles off precariously with his wife in the other direction, ignored by the cameras.

For new generations of Mississippians the past is an un-fathomable, irrevocable inheritance. A high school student growing up in Natchez will undoubtedly hear of a place in town once called the Forks of the Road Slave Market. On a visit to the spot of the slave market, he will find only a shuttered bar, a parking lot, and a small kiosk. The sign on the kiosk explains that here once stood the second largest slave market in the South, second only to the one in New Orleans. From 1830 to 1863 up to five hundred slaves could be sold at the market on a given day. The student might try to picture the scene of humans in shackles being herded on stage for sale, and the image would make him shudder. This is his hometown, where he goes to school, where generations of his family have lived, the one place in the world where he belongs. He hears the word "nig-ger" a lot from older people, but neither he nor his friends use it. He's never done anything mean to black kids—although he does attend an all-white school. He feels bad about what happened, but it also seems a little unfair to him, the vague sense that he needs to account for it. Somehow, this past is his past, and he wonders what it means about who he is and who he could become.

CHAPTER 14

Kathy Nester has earned a reputation in Jackson as a dedicated liberal and first-class civil rights lawyer, so her friends were somewhat shocked to see her representing James Ford Seale. Although she refused to give interviews to the press, a couple of her friends talked to the *Clarion-Ledger*. The resulting article implied that even though Nester must utterly detest her client, she would do her best to defend him. The article quoted the lawyer who represented Byron De La Beckwith in the 1994 trial as saying that he was driving from Oxford to Jackson when he learned that he had been appointed to represent the notorious Klansman. The idea literally made him sick, and he had to pull over and throw up on the side of the road. Obviously, Seale, like De La Beckwith, must be guilty. The article makes it sound like Nester will put up a good fight but doesn't expect—and maybe doesn't really want—to win.

The article couldn't be further from the truth. Nester is convinced the government can't prove that Seale was involved in the kidnapping and murder of Dee and Moore. If a black man were on trial for murdering a white man with this sort of evidence, the civil rights community would be in an uproar. Charles Marcus Edwards is a flat-out liar, and he's lying to this day, and without him, the government has nothing. Except of course that her client was a Klansman and therefore part of the "reign of terror." Hell, back then the government itself was a part of the "reign of terror."

Nester expected to encounter a monster in her client. Instead, she found Seale to be a congenial, thoughtful man. He treated her and the defense staff with courtesy and respect. He said funny things, like someone was "lower than sweat on a worm." He was not educated, but he seemed to have good common sense. She fought hard to get him released on bail pending the trial because of his poor health, but the government resisted, and the judge wasn't having it. She was worried that he wouldn't survive the trial.

Nester has fought hard from the beginning, but with little success. She filed a motion for change of venue to Natchez and lost. She filed a motion for disclosure of confidential informants and lost. She filed a motion to suppress Seale's supposed confession and lost. She filed a motion to prohibit the use of a racially loaded jury questionnaire and lost. She filed motions to dismiss for spoliation of evidence and lack of a speedy trial, and she lost. There's one motion she lost which might be her ace in the hole if her client is convicted: a motion to dismiss because the indictment was outside the statute of limitations.

According to the statute under which Seale was charged, kidnapping was a capital offense in 1964, meaning that it carried the death penalty. Under a separate statute, capital crimes were not subject to a statute of limitations. However,

in 1968 the Supreme Court ruled the death penalty provision in the kidnapping statute unconstitutional, which
meant that the statute under which Seale was charged
no longer carried the death penalty. In 1972 Congress
amended the statute to exclude it as a capital offense.
Nester argued that the amendment was retroactive, and
therefore the charges in this case were subject to the normal
five-year statute of limitations. Nester is convinced Judge
Wingate was wrong in refusing her motion to dismiss on
this ground.

Nester knew the government intended to offer the
statement of Klan leader and FBI informant Ernest Gilbert, who had died in 2004. The government wanted it in
so the entire case wouldn't stand or fall on Edwards. She
also knew if the statement got in, Seale was finished.

In fact, there was some ambivalence on the government
side about seeking the admission of Gilbert's statement.
As damning as the statement was, it was clearly hearsay
and, if admitted, could set up strong grounds for reversal
on appeal. In the beginning, Fitzgerald was so opposed to
using the statement that she threatened to withdraw from
the case if the government tried to introduce it. Attorneys
in Lampton's office eventually convinced her of the viabil-
ity of a particular legal theory for its admission.

Although the Sixth Amendment to the Constitution
guarantees a defendant's right to confront witnesses against
him, the courts have held that a defendant cannot be heard
to complain about his inability to cross-examine a witness
when the defendant himself is responsible for the witness's
unavailability. The principle is called the rule of forfei-
ture. The most obvious example is when the defendant has

murdered the witness whose statement the government now seeks to introduce. A refusal to testify for fear of reprisal fits within this rule. Gilbert refused to testify for forty years, the government insists, because he feared Seale would kill him.

At a hearing before the trial, Angela Givens, the sole black lawyer in the case, argued the issue for the government. She pointed to evidence showing that the Seales suspected Gilbert of being an informant and had specifically threatened to kill him and that the Seales had murdered at least one person whom they believed to be an informant. One former FBI agent described the Seales as such dangerous killers they were even feared by their fellow Klansmen.

Nester argued that Gilbert had voluntarily appeared on ABC's *20/20* in 2000 and revealed his identity as an informer, so whatever fear he might have had of the Seales and the Klan was nullified at that point. He lived for three years without any harm coming to him, during which time the government could have brought the case.

At a hearing prior to trial, Judge Wingate agreed with Nester: once Gilbert's identity had been revealed on *20/20*, it was up to the government to provide a judicial forum for his testimony. His statement would be excluded.

Now, just as U.S. Attorney Lampton had feared, there was only one arrow remaining in the government's quiver, and it was Charles Marcus Edwards, Seale's fellow Klansman, kidnapper, conspirator, and killer and a confessed liar many times over. And what the court would hear about Edwards would be far worse than what had been reported in the press. The government would corroborate his statement in as many ways as it could, but it would only take one juror to say, hell, we can't convict on nothing but that liar's testimony, and hang the jury.

As for Nester, Gilbert's statement was so clearly inadmissible that winning its exclusion didn't feel like much of a victory.

CHAPTER 15

Finally, the jury is selected. Eight whites and four blacks, a racial makeup about right for the judicial district. Only two people on the jury were alive when the killings happened. Gone are the racists, black and white, those who thought it a waste to prosecute an old man, those with a relative in the Klan, and those who started off thinking Seale owed them an explanation. Most have seen *Mississippi Burning*. None admit that it will affect their judgment.

On the day of opening statements, Seale is not alone. Directly behind him is his current wife, Jeannie. Next to her sit her daughter, Carolyn, and her son-in-law. Behind them are several of her relatives. But not one of Seale's blood relations is present: neither of his two living brothers, none of his three children, and none of his many grandchildren.

Although the jail in Madison, an affluent suburb north of Jackson, is a good two hours from Roxie, Jeannie, who doesn't drive, visits her husband as often as she can. She worries about the medical treatment he's receiving. She was taking him to three different doctors and giving him ten pills daily when he was arrested, and now he needs oxygen twenty-four hours a day. Those cops showed up in four cars at 1:30 A.M., and they lied on the stand when they said they read him his rights before taking him away. They even watched him through the door as he went to the bathroom.

Jeannie was born in Hattiesburg but moved to the country outside Roxie in 1950. Her brother introduced her to James at the White Apple Baptist Church in 1994, and she married him a year later. They live in a motor home on her daughter and son-in-law's property outside Roxie. She swears she had never heard a thing about the murders of those boys before meeting James, or even afterward, until the law showed up at their door. She has never even heard James use the word "nigger." "He never denigrates blacks. His best friend is a black man."

Jeannie knows the rumors that James killed his first wife, Shirley, but doesn't believe a word. Shirley, whom James had married when they were eighteen, was manic-depressive. One day, James went to the store, and when he came back, he found Shirley had blowed her head off with a shotgun. Simple as that. Jeannie's daughter, Carolyn, loves Mr. James, as she calls him, as if he were her father. Carolyn cried when she saw him enter the courtroom in cuffs and leg irons that first day.

Jeannie isn't surprised that James's children haven't shown up in court. James Junior told her that he couldn't go to the trial because he had to get along with blacks at the automotive plant in Alabama where he worked. A son-in-law explained that he and his wife couldn't put up bail because they had just spent $70,000 on a new house. A daughter said she couldn't get time off work. She figures the truth is, none of them want their pictures in the paper.

"James Seale is a kind, Christian man," Jeannie insists. "He only tells the truth. He would never have done what they said."

ACT II

CHAPTER 16

The trial of J. W. Milam and Roy Bryant for the murder of Emmett Till took place in the small town of Sumner, one of two seats of Tallahatchie County, in the heart of the Delta. Emmett Till was abducted from his great uncle Mose Wright's home outside of the small town of Money in Leflore County. Most thinking is that Emmett was murdered in Leflore County, tied to a cotton gin fan, and dumped in the Tallahatchie River. The problem, from Sumner's point of view, is that his body came to the surface on its side of the river, thereby resulting in the trial being held in its courthouse and bringing enduring notoriety to the small community. To this day, white residents of Sumner resent the national publicity the trial brought to their doorstep. They insist no one in their town would ever have committed such a terrible crime.

Once the trial ended in 1955 and the publicity died down, Till's murder was seldom spoken of in either the white or black community. Jerome Little, fifty-seven, a black county supervisor who grew up the son of sharecroppers and is now, after a career as a prison guard at Parchman, one of the most powerful men in the county, never

heard the story of Emmett Till as a boy. The long commu-
nal silence might have stemmed from different sources—
the whites wanted no reminder of the murder, and the
blacks, if they did know about it, saw only trouble rising
from talking about it—but the silence was pervasive.

Since Reconstruction days, Sumner has always had
more black than white residents, and currently the ratio is
about 80 to 20 percent. Charleston, the other county seat,
is predominantly white. Like many towns in the Delta, the
blacks in Sumner have the votes and the political power,
but the whites still own the land and the banks.

Although Sumner appears somewhat prosperous because of its courthouse and attendant businesses, the town
is caught in the same economic mire of lousy schools and
joblessness as the rest of the Delta. In 2006 Little was
brainstorming with several state legislators about ways to
bring money into the county, when one of them said, hell,
Jerome, you've got a great thing right there in Sumner:
the courthouse where the Emmett Till murder trial took
place. Little, a large man with a loud voice that rises in
pitch when he gets excited, has well-honed political
instincts, and he got the idea. Within days, he formed an
Emmett Till Commission. He envisioned a major event:
there would be a press conference, with officials from all
levels of government attending; the Till family would
come to accept the regrets of the community and to celebrate the plans for the Emmett Till Museum.

But Little understood that if the project were to have a
chance of getting off the ground, the whites in town would
have to be brought onboard. More than that, the blacks
and whites would need to work together, something that

had never happened in Tallahatchie County. Little knew that winning the support of Frank Mitchener, one of the wealthiest plantation owners in the county and on whose plantation he had grown up the son of sharecroppers, would be critical. He also knew that Betty Pearson, the daughter and wife of wealthy plantation owners and one of the few whites in the county he felt he could trust, would have to be on the commission. They would encounter considerable resistance from both the black and white communities, and each would need its own motivation to support the project. For the blacks, it was an Emmett Till Museum, perhaps an apology, and some money coming in. For the whites, it would have to be something different.

Betty Pearson is a slight, silver-haired woman in her mid-eighties with crystal blue eyes and a frank, engaging manner. She's a rare character in Mississippi: a planter-class liberal. She frankly admits her parents were racists; they believed that white people were superior to black people. They took good care of the blacks on their plantation, but treated them like children.

Pearson attended segregated schools in Sumner, went to Ole Miss, and when her father refused permission for her to attend Columbia University in New York, she joined the Marine Corps and served in World War II. She returned home to marry a planter, Bill Pearson, and raise a family. Since then, she's spent much of her life working for equal rights for blacks. She served on the Mississippi Advisory Commission to the U.S. Civil Rights Commission, which her father called an act of betrayal. She's endured more than one voice on the phone calling her a nigger lover and threatening harm to her and her family.

But even today, although Pearson has had blacks to her home for lunch, she wouldn't invite them to a cocktail party or formal dinner. They just wouldn't fit in with her crowd. She also wouldn't have put her children in Sumner's public schools when they were integrated in 1969. They would have been the only three white kids in the school. If all the white residents hadn't pulled their kids out of the schools, it would have been different.

Pearson was thirty-three when the Till trial took place. Over the objection of the sheriff, who thought the trial was no place for a lady, she attended all five days of it. The jurors were all white men, rednecks like J. W. Milam and Roy Bryant, people she had no use for. (The jurors were selected from a list of registered voters, and there were no blacks registered in Tallahatchie County in 1955.) In the courtroom, the whites sat on the benches, and the blacks stood in the back. The white reporters sat at a table inside the bar; the black reporters and Mrs. Till sat at a table off to themselves. Milam and Bryant sat in straw-backed rockers and smirked and joked throughout the trial. Their kids, little cowboys, shot their cap pistols and climbed rowdily over the benches and railings during the proceedings.

Pearson was ashamed of her community: every lawyer in town worked for the defense; jars were set up on store counters to collect money for the legal fees. Counsel insisted in court that there was no proof that the body was actually Emmett Till. The sheriff testified that he couldn't even tell if the body was black or white or what had caused the death. When Till's mother took the stand and identified the ring found on the body as having belonged to the boy's father, the defense argued that the ring had been planted there by the NAACP. The lawyers even argued that Emmett Till was still alive in Chicago.

Mose Wright, from whose house Emmett Till was taken, was what, in those days, Pearson called an old-timey Negro, a darky. He did something Pearson doubted she would ever see: he stood up in a court of law and pointed the finger of guilt at two white men. But the jury was back in an hour; one of the jurors was heard to joke that they would have been back sooner, except they'd stopped for Cokes. She never heard mention of Emmett Till or the trial after the acquittals.

The white community soon found a motivation for getting onboard the Till memorial project: the restoration of the Sumner courthouse to its condition at the time of the trial in 1955. Charleston, the other county seat, was far wealthier and whiter than Sumner and it had a larger and more impressive courthouse. Charleston would love nothing more than to see its rival courthouse fall into such disrepair as to be closed down; it would then be the one and only county seat of Tallahatchie County. Which would finish Sumner.

The two motivations fit perfectly: restoring the courthouse to its condition in 1955 would not only enhance the effort to restore the history of the trial and Emmett Till but preserve the historic building itself.

Not all whites in the Delta see things the way Betty Pearson does. Some believe that blacks in the larger Delta towns have no desire for change. One educated, middle-aged white professional, who had lived and worked in the town of Greenville for twenty years, moved away recently in disgust and started over in a "hill town." The way he sees it, younger whites leave for school and jobs and don't come back, and as the older white people retire, they set out for more comfortable surroundings, like northeastern Mississippi. Greenville is now 80 percent black, and although the whites might still have most of the money, it's the blacks who make the rules. Three of five county supervisors and city councilmen are black, as are the sheriff, the town clerk, and the tax collector. There's only one white judge in the city. Greenville, in this man's mind, has essentially turned into a welfare state. It all comes down to education and the work ethic, both of which are missing in that town. It's why educated whites like himself are leaving, and why they'll keep on leaving.

As for the old Klan cases, the professional shakes his head. Murder cases should be tried if the evidence is there, but at some point it's got to end. These cases just serve to keep reminding every one of the past. Big deal. The rest of the world doesn't care about Mississippi. Most blacks don't care about those old Klansmen. It's the media, the papers, that drive it. People like it here in Mississippi. They live here because they choose to.

CHAPTER 17

A trial is a drama of competing stories of guilt and innocence played out before a chorus. In the end, the chorus
decides which story is best and declares it to be the truth.
So the lawyers are essentially storytellers: each presents
his story in the opening statement, lays out the "facts" to
support it, then returns in the closing argument to repeat
his story and rip holes in the other side's. All storytellers
are salesmen, and good trial lawyers are no different;
they're selling themselves as well as their stories.

There are always subtexts in the play, the stories behind
the story. You want the chorus—the jury—to identify with
your story, so you look for a theme the jury can relate to.
Then you blow it up until it almost becomes bigger than
the story itself: discrimination, greed, injustice, racism, ex-
ploitation, self-preservation, law and order. Here in the
federal courtroom in Jackson, Mississippi, the driving
story behind the story is redemption. Redemption not of a
person but of a state, of a culture.

Redemption can't be mentioned in the telling of the
story—if the prosecutor were to spell it out, she would im-
properly suggest to the jury that its role was something

other than that of fact finder, and on the other side, Nester has done what she can to drive it from the jurors' minds in voir dire, assuming the risk of only impressing it more deeply—but it is as present in the courtroom as the defendant himself. No one mentions De La Beckwith, Bowers, Killen, or Avants, and not every juror might be able to link up the names with the crimes, but their sins are the collective sins of every (white) Mississippian. Seale, the subtext goes, is the latest in the line of these murdering Klansmen, and the redemption train is leaving the station for him, just like it did for each of them.

The countersubtext likewise cannot be spoken and unfortunately for the defense, it is nowhere near as powerful. Here's a sick old man, at the end of his days, who, even if he did the crime, might well have reformed and led a good Christian life. Isn't it a little late to go back and punish him forty-three years after the fact? Doesn't everyone deserve a second chance? The counter-countersubtext to this is that he's only got a few years left, so we're not really able to make him pay the way he made those boys pay.

Nester's only chance is to force—or persuade—the jury to twist its lens down to a very narrow focus. All the government really has against her client is the word of a self-confessed liar, but she doesn't really have much of her own story—nothing like an alibi or evidence of a more likely suspect. Her basic story is that the prosecution's story isn't worth a damn. Certainly not convincing beyond a reasonable doubt.

The judge has the near-impossible task of convincing the jurors that from this moment forward, the reality in this room is the only reality that counts, that they must play by his rules and his rules alone, that they are to leave the outside world behind, including all their biases and prejudices and feelings and be completely here. The judge is also the stage director who decides what facts of the drama can be shown the jury and which can't. In the end, his task is, like Moses, to pronounce the law, which the jury then applies to the facts it has so impartially and unemotionally ascertained.

What effect the judge's being a black man will have on the jury is a great imponderable. He comes across as a caring but strict father figure, one whom you would want to please, and his presence on the bench is certainly a stark reminder of how much things have changed since the crimes here before him were committed. One wonders if the jury will feel bad for him, and therefore vengeful toward the defendant, when the word "nigger" is used and stories told about all the horrible things that whites inflicted on blacks in those times. One wonders if a juror would be a little more hesitant to acquit a white man of a crime against a black man in front of a black judge.

Seale seems to grow less substantial with every passing day. He enters from a far door to the right of the bench, and he walks carefully across the room, bony chest stuck out like the prow of a boat, eyes cast down to avoid tripping on cords. Approaching the counsel table, he gives a weak smile to his wife and her family. She waves back and leans forward as if to touch him. As the judge reads the charges again to the jury, now that they are sworn in, in the same staccato W-K-K-K-K, his wife presses her hand to her mouth in horror at the litany of gruesome specifics.

Maybe the possibility that she loves a monster has begun to seep into her mind.

Fitzgerald is first on stage. Dressed in a black suit with a modest string of pearls, thick ash-blonde hair perfectly coiffed, lips a bright red, she is the picture of professional elegance. She moves efficiently and seems well organized. She is courteous to everyone, flashes a wonderfully warm smile, and still projects a feeling of being slightly danger-ous. She has a typed statement, and she glances at it as she paces. Finally, Judge Wingate nods, and the play begins.

The faces of Charles Eddie Moore and Henry Hezekiah Dee appear on the monitors in front of the jurors and on each counsel table. Dee, described as having smooth, dark skin and white teeth and being a dapper dresser, is glancing over his shoulder with a slight smile. Dee was the first one to ask a girl to dance, the guy with the best moves on the floor. He had been raised by his grandmother and sent to stay with an aunt in Chicago in the fall of 1962. He had a little trouble with the rules of the household and returned to Roxie in February 1963. There had been no known photo of Henry Dee until a few weeks earlier, when a resi-dent in Meadville found one buried in a trunk. The find is a blessing for the prosecution: victims need to have a face; they need to come to life before they are killed.

Next to Dee, looking warmly out at the audience, is Charles Moore. Charles has a broad forehead and his eyes, tilting slightly down at the outer edges, are open and in-telligent. A success story in the making. He was voted pres-ident of his freshman, sophomore, and senior classes, the best dressed and most intelligent of his senior class at Lillie

May Bryant School in Bude. He played center on the football team, under the hands of his older brother, Thomas, the quarterback. On his application to Alcorn State, Moore wrote that he wanted to be a teacher because he liked helping people learn. He said that he had recently read Margaret Walker Alexander's "For My People," Charles Darwin's *Origin of the Species*, and John F. Kennedy's *Profiles in Courage*. The latter was his favorite because "it had so much to do with the struggle of an individual in his development, and struggling impressed me greatly." After his brief suspension from Alcorn for protesting cafeteria conditions, he had received a letter readmitting him. He was coming of age at the very height of the civil rights movement in Mississippi.

At the lectern, Fitzgerald addresses the jurors, who glance back and forth between her and the photos. She begins where she must, with the crime itself. She tells a story the world does not know, and it horrifies even the most jaded. On May 2, 1964, Charles Moore stood on the bank of the Mississippi River and watched as James Ford Seale and Jack Seale chained Henry Dee to an engine block. Charles watched as the defendant and his brother took Henry to the boat and rowed out into the river; he watched as they rolled his friend, alive and breathing, over the edge; and he watched as they came back to shore for him. The defendant and a third Klansman then chained Moore to rails, took him to the boat, rowed out in the water, and rolled him over the edge to join his friend at the bottom of the river. Unable all the while to cry out or struggle because this defendant, James Ford Seale, had taped his hands together and his mouth shut.

Fitzgerald lets the image of Charles Moore watching his friend being pushed over the edge of the boat slowly expand until you can almost see it in the air in front of her, and then she tells the jury that the youths were next seen in July when one of their bodies surfaced "headless and rotted after two months in the water."

Fitzgerald moves on to Charles Marcus Edwards: he will say that during the beating in the forest he asked the boys if they were "right with the Lord" because he knew even then what their end would be. You will learn that the boys confessed in the woods that there were guns stored in the First Baptist Church in Roxie and that Edwards, Clyde Seale, and Curtis Dunn left the forest to get the sheriff to search the church. The government must prove that the defendant and others kidnapped the boys, took them across state lines, and murdered them, and you will learn that Edwards knows in great detail what happened to the boys after they were taken from the woods. And you will learn why, despite his participation in the crime, you should believe his story and convict the defendant. Fitzgerald closes with Seale's 1964 "confession" to the agents who arrested him; she repeats it almost in a stage whisper: "Yes, but I'm not going to admit it. You're going to have to prove it." Which she now intends to do.

Seale, who stared casually at a spot on the wall behind the judge as Fitzgerald spoke, tracks defense co-counsel George Lucas as he rises and crosses the room to the podium. Lucas delivers a very brief, almost folksy opening for the defense, beginning by stating how sorry he, Nester, and his client are for what happened to those two young men. But where is the credible evidence that James Seale had anything to do with it? Everything Edwards is going to tell you he could have learned other ways. You can't believe him. You might not like what you hear about Seale, but it is not a crime to be a racist or a member of the Klan. This time was a terrible chapter in the state's history, Lucas says. He hopes for the families' sake the crime can be resolved, but you cannot set aside the law to make the families feel better. It's all Lucas could say, really, but it seems lacking in passion and it bleaches little of the vividness from Fitzgerald's terrible image.

Fitzgerald calls her first witness. John Rogan tells his story on the stand like he's rehearsed it his whole life. He was only nineteen at the time and had just started working at the funeral home in Tallulah—he's been a professional undertaker ever since—when he got the call that there was a body in the Palmyra chute of the Mississippi River. Rogan grabbed some gloves and a body bag and took off. He and two other men rowed out in the chute, which was high from the June rise. In the middle of the river, he spotted a backbone protruding from a pair of jeans, resting up against a half-submerged log. The task of retrieving the body was left up to him, the kid—and when he grabbed what there was of it, one of the feet fell off. He handled the corpse as gently as he could while getting it into the body bag. He spotted an *M* on the belt buckle and wondered if it might be Mickey Schwerner. On shore, the men didn't take the body out of the boat but just put the boat on the trailer and hauled it to the coroner's office in Vidalia, where the FBI was waiting.

Fitzgerald calls a game warden, who is so ancient and disoriented that he looks up to the speakers in the corners of the ceiling in search of the person behind the voice addressing him. Fitzgerald gently calls to him—"Sir, I'm over here"—until he eventually locates her behind the lectern. The warden tells a slightly different story: a fisherman's wife snagged the vertebrae with a fishing pole and tugged the body to the surface. The next day the warden went out in a boat with an FBI agent looking for a second body, which they found fifty yards down river. This body was largely intact, although very rancid. (His memory failed him here; only the bottom half of Dee was found.) A film clip shows a man poking the loose body on the river's edge with a stick, then struggling to gently wrap a body bag around it. The witness wobbles from the stand, proud to be of service after all these years but happy to be done.

CHAPTER 18

The trial's second day begins on a less gruesome but equally sad note as family and friends of the victims take the stand. The prosecution calls Erbie Bell Shaw, a cousin of Moore's who lived in Bude and with whose family Moore stayed when he was in high school. Shaw testifies that Moore had attended a May Day party at the school in Bude on Friday night and then spent the night at her house. The last time she saw him was the next morning, when, dressed in a Banlon sweater and blue jeans and wearing a Bulova watch, he left the house for Roxie.

Joey Rollins identifies the photo of Henry Dee and says that his hairdo, slicked back like a lady's, was not a popular style in Meadville those days. He saw Henry and Charles in the store in Meadville on Saturday morning, and they talked about maybe meeting some girls at a dance in Bude that night. He never saw his friends again.

Thelma Collins, one of Dee's sisters, testifies that she first learned her brother was missing when Mazie Moore, Charles's mother, called and asked if the boys were with her. Later, the authorities called and said her brother's remains had been found. She went to Jackson to identify him, but there was nothing left of him, she explains in tears, but a bag of bones.

After an ancient FBI agent, who seems to drift off during his answers, testifies at length about the unsuccessful effort to link the serial number on the engine block and the chains and the rails to the Klansmen, Fitzgerald announces matter-of-factly that the government is now calling Charles Marcus Edwards. One might think she would save the big gun until much later in the trial, when more of the foundation of the crime had been laid—the recovery of the rest of the bodies or Seale's confession—but Fitzgerald apparently wants her star witness out of the shadows and into the light before much more of the story unfolds.

Edwards seems like an ordinary guy: average height, five feet, nine inches, a little stocky at 195 pounds, hazel eyes, thick, graying mustache. (The muscled, thuggish look from his 1964 booking photo is long gone.) Born in Franklin County in 1933, Edwards quit school after the eleventh grade to enlist in the Dixie Division of the Mississippi National Guard. He fought in Korea, and survived the battle of Pork Chop Hill. He returned home, married, had four kids, and spent the next forty-five years working at the International Paper Company in Natchez.

Edwards was surprised when Jim Ingram and Agent Bill Stokes showed up on his doorstep in July 2006. Ingram explained that the Fifth Amendment, which protects a person from self-incrimination, no longer applied to him regarding the events of May 2, 1964. The protections had been stripped away by order of Judge Henry Wingate in return for a promise from the government that anything

Edwards said could never be used against him in court. The government was going to put Edwards in front of a grand jury to talk about Moore and Dee, and he could not refuse to answer questions on the grounds that he might incriminate himself because, by law, he no longer could incriminate himself. Unless he failed to tell the truth, in which case the statements could be used against him and he could be prosecuted for perjury.

It shook Edwards up. He knew what the men wanted: James Ford Seale. Not that he and Seale had been close during the past few decades—in fact, Edwards still considered Seale a dangerous man—but he had taken the Klan oath of secrecy before God in 1964.

Edwards and his attorney Max Graves met with Ingram and Stokes in Graves's office a few days later. Edwards told a much larger story than he had told the FBI forty-two years earlier. He said that he had joined the Klan in 1964, and in the spring of that year there was talk at a Klan meeting about the Black Panthers (no longer the Muslims) running guns into Franklin County. He told the others that Dee was a likely member of the Black Panthers because he wore a "stocking rag" on his head. A few days later, Edwards was working in his garden when Clyde Seale, Archie Prather, and Curtis Dunn showed up and told him James Seale had spotted Dee in town at the bank and was keeping an eye on him. The men went into town and observed Seale pick up the boys in his white Volkswagen. They followed Seale into the forest, where Dee and Moore denied knowing anything about the guns. James Seale, Dunn, and Edwards began whipping them with switches.

Then Edwards added a few more facts: after about fifteen minutes of whipping, the boys said the guns were

stored at the First Baptist Church of Roxie. This made
sense to the Klansmen because they knew Preacher Briggs
had been stirring up trouble in the black community. Edwards suggested they go to town, get the sheriff, and search
the church. Edwards, Clyde Seale, Dunn, and Prather
rounded up Sheriff Hutto and Patrolman Beasley, and they
drove to the church. Edwards was left on the road to stand
guard while the others went inside. When the search failed
to turn up any guns, Mr. Clyde took Edwards home. Edwards told the agents that he only learned what had happened to Dee and Moore through the news media and that
he had never talked about that day with James Seale or
anyone else.

To U.S. Attorney Dunn Lampton, the search of the
church explained for the first time why the Klan killed
Dee and Moore. If the boys had lived and told authorities
about their kidnapping and beating, the fact of the search
would have corroborated their story. All of the perpetra-
tors, including Hutto and Beasley (who not surprisingly
never mentioned the search in any of their many statements to the FBI), would then have been put in serious
jeopardy.

This latest version, however, still did not bring Seale
into play. The government had nothing more than it had
before. Lampton was convinced Edwards knew the rest of
the story. Seale and the others would have talked about it,
probably more than once, and Edwards would likely have
been there. On May 3, the day after Dee and Moore disappeared, a few of the Bunkley Klan arrived in a truck at
Edwards's house on Kirby Road and announced they were
moving him to a ramshackle house on Bunkley Road. Edwards went along with the move because he was scared the

black community might retaliate against his family. Sometime in the next few days, or weeks, or months, he had to have heard the story of what happened after the beating in the forest.

The prosecution team, now including Fitzgerald and a second attorney from Justice, Eric Gibson, decided that Ingram and Stokes should make another run at Edwards. In this interview, Edwards added a few new facts to the "truth": Seale always carried a sawed-off shotgun in his car, and he had it with him on May 2. Seale held this shotgun on Dee and Moore while the others beat them. Dee and Moore specifically said the guns were kept in the baptistery of the church. This time it was Mr. Clyde, not Edwards, who said they needed to go get the guns. At the church, they met a black man who unlocked a side door for the searchers. But Edwards continued to insist that none of the others told him of Dee and Moore's "final disposition."

The government team sat Edwards down with his lawyer and told him they didn't think he was telling the truth and reminded him that he could be prosecuted if he lied in front of the grand jury. They asked if he would be willing to take a lie detector test. They assured him that if he passed the test, they would not hassle him further.

If Edwards had held his ground and refused to take the test, the game would have been up. The government had no way to prove he was lying, so the threat of a perjury prosecution was an empty one. But Edwards, for whatever reason and with his lawyer's concurrence, agreed to the polygraph, and the game was on.

Edwards went into a room alone with the FBI polygraph expert. The agent ran him through a series of questions, then told him he had answered truthfully on all but one: whether he had ever been told by anyone what happened to Moore and Dee after leaving the forest. The agent then threatened trouble for Edwards and his family if he didn't tell the truth. The mention of his family did the trick: Edwards wrote out a statement saying that Seale had indeed told him what had happened to Dee and Moore after the beating in the forest. On November 4, Edwards gave a more formal statement.

Edwards said that James Ford Seale told him shortly after the murder that he and Curtis Dunn had taken Moore and Dee from the forest to Clyde Seale's farm. There, Clyde Seale, back from the search, called Jack Seale and Ernest Parker, who joined him and the others at the farm. They lined the trunk of Parker's red car with plastic, gave the youths cigarettes, then taped the boys' hands and mouths and put them in the trunk of the car. James and Jack Seale and Ernest Parker drove across the bridge at Natchez, into Louisiana, and north to Parker's Island. There, the men secured Dee to the engine block, and James and Jack Seale rowed him out in the river and pushed him overboard. The two Seales returned to shore, attached iron weights to Moore, and James Seale and Parker rowed him out in the water and pushed him overboard.

Edwards attended a Klan meeting that night at which Clyde Seale told him that Dee and Moore had been "disposed of," which he understood to mean murdered. Edwards told his wife everything he knew about the murders.

CHAPTER 19

Edwards was no hero in Meadville. Well before the trial, everyone in the small town of 550 understood that he had caused all the excitement by ratting on Seale. The publicity had brought the town—the entire county—to grief once again. It made no sense: the blacks had gotten the right to vote, the schools were integrated—of the eighteen members of the Bulldogs 2007 football team, which made it to the finals, fifteen were black, as were seven of the nine cheerleaders—but more than that, there was peace in the county. There was an understanding that seemed to suit everyone. Blacks and whites worked together, fished together, hung out together, but they didn't go to each others' houses for dinner, they didn't gather at the same church on Sunday—the Baptist and Methodist churches in town are either all black or all white—and the kids didn't go to high school proms together or marry each other.

The chairman of the Board of County Supervisors, the most powerful position in the county, is black, and whites in Franklin County will swear he treats everyone fair and square, regardless of their race. White lawyers have black clients; white doctors treat black patients. In Bude, some blacks live comfortably in previously all-white neighbor-hoods. Racial incidents are a thing of the past. In their own southern, post–Jim Crow manner, blacks and whites in Franklin County treat each other with respect, civility, and even affection. It's the way it is.

And yet, in Franklin County, as in all of Mississippi, race is everywhere and nowhere. Like the constant buzz of a fading florescent light, it's always there. The Franklin County Museum, in Meadville, chronicles the county's history since the turn of the nineteenth century. The museum walls are covered with pictures of the Bank of Roxie in 1904, picnics at Roxie High School, a group of Civilian Conservation Corp workers, hunting clubs, students, and beauty-contest winners. Not a single photo contains the face of a black man, woman, or child. No pictures of the black high school, or civic clubs, or churches. The only representation of blacks is a colorful painting of a cotton field in which blacks with burlap sacks on their backs are picking cotton. But no one seems to mind. It is what it is: a museum of white Franklin County history.

The contrast between Meadville, where two black youths were kidnapped, and Sumner, where the murderers of Emmett Till were tried and acquitted, is striking. Even during the sixties, Sumner kept itself free of racial inci-dents and turmoil. The community was only too well aware that an incident such as a lynching or a whipping could bring the civil rights activists to town with reporters in tow, and all sorts of social disruption would result. Sum-ner kept its head down, its voice low. It just failed to do things, like installing adequate sewer lines in the black community. Meadville, on the other hand, went straight at it: the Klan basically ran Franklin County in the sixties, and it enforced Jim Crow with the lash and the bullet. Now, Meadville maintains a museum dedicated to white history, while Sumner raises money to build a museum to honor Emmett Till.

Max Graves, Edwards's primary attorney, believes that there is still "us and them" in Mississippi. There will always be "us and them." This is the Deep South, and try as they might, northerners will never understand it. Graves believes firmly that very few people in Franklin County, black or white, wanted the Moore-Dee case resurrected. Dredging it up meant having to relive the past and suffer all the old feelings.

The disruption of the peace in Mississippi came as it always did—from the federal government and the media. The old bitterness, stemming from the earliest days of the civil rights effort, from the Civil War, from the days before the Civil War when northerners refused to return fugitive slaves, came seeping back to the surface in southwest Mississippi over the Seale case. People were upset by the way the arrest of James Ford Seale was handled. The feds, who had a press release all ready to go, made it look like Meadville had been protecting and covering up for the murderers of these two boys for the past forty-three years. The news stories implied that the town had told whoever asked about Seale that he was dead and that he'd only recently been found to be alive. Which was bullshit—anybody in the county could have told you James Ford Seale was living in an RV a few blocks off the highway outside of Roxie.

In the days after Seale's arrest, the national media reported over and over that he was a deputy sheriff in Franklin County, which was also wrong. Sheriff James Newman himself called up one of the reporters and ripped him over it: How hard would it have been to call the sheriff's office and ask, does James Seale work there? Has he ever worked there? People in the county were pissed, and the sheriff had to work at calming them down. The locals saw it as Dunn Lampton, a Mississippian turned fed, creating a media frenzy for the publicity. As if people didn't already see Mississippi as the armpit of the country. What really burned the sheriff was that the feds could have solved the murders forty years ago, but, as he says, "putting it in layman's terms, one FBI informant was worth more than two dead niggers."

No, Charles Marcus Edwards is not a popular man in Meadville or Franklin County. All this mess has been stirred up because of him, he's just as guilty as Seale, and that's the way a lot of people in the county feel about it.

Jeannie Seale, the defendant's wife, finds some satisfaction in Edwards's status as a pariah. She's never met the man, but she's heard that people won't talk to him, that they will even cross the street to avoid him. Edwards fooled people for a long time; why, even James didn't believe her when she told him Edwards was going to testify against him. "He wouldn't do that," James said.

To lawyer Graves, an inveterate pipe smoker who claims a passing acquaintanceship with William Faulkner, Edwards is not a complicated man. He may well be naïve and too trusting, but he is not evil. The way Edwards saw it in 1964, life was getting damn scary. A war was coming to Southwest Mississippi, like the one he had fought in Korea, except this one was on his home ground. Malcolm X was preaching blacks against whites, blacks had got the vote, black fists were being pumped in the air at the Olympics, and right here in Franklin County, guns were being run in for a black insurrection. The hot-blooded young men decided to resist—black people were going to rise up and attack, so why not get the first lick in?

In Graves's view, Edwards was never a true Klansman. This—the taking of the two boys—was the only Klan violence he was ever involved in, and he couldn't have known in the beginning that it was going to result in the boys' murder. Hell, the Dee boy only lived a ways down the road from Edwards, and he had given him rides to and from town many times. Edwards was under the influence of the group, particularly Mr. Clyde and Mr. Arch (Prather), who had raised him. He just went along.

CHAPTER 20

Paige Fitzgerald had presented Edwards to the federal grand jury in October 2006. The critical goal in this preliminary chamber was to tie him down on the facts so he couldn't wiggle out of them later, when the indictment was issued and the spotlight fell on him and he might have second thoughts. She needed to nail him into a corner so that if he changed his story, he would be admitting to having lied to the grand jury, which meant his immunity would be gone and he could be prosecuted for what he had said there. She wanted him to keep this possibility in mind when the rest of the world—his community, family, and friends—learned of what he had done.

Edwards told the grand jury how the murders came about: At one of the Bunkley Klan meetings a few weeks earlier, when the men were talking about the Muslim guns and the upcoming black insurrection, it was decided that the only way to find the guns was to pick up and interrogate a local Negro. But who? Edwards gave them a name: Henry Hezekiah Dee. Not only had Dee been to Chicago, but he wore a black bandana around his head, like the Black Panthers. To the Bunkley Klan, it made perfect sense that the guns were coming from Chicago, the home away from home for Mississippi blacks, and who better to know where the weapons were stored than a local black who had just returned from Chicago?

It's not hard to believe that Edwards didn't initially realize what he had done at the meeting—marked Dee for death and himself for perdition—but as the truck slowed to a stop in front of the bank and he identified the Dee boy to Mr. Clyde and Mr. Arch with a nod, he must have realized what fate now awaited the youths. He knew the violent reputation of the Seale men. When the Klan finally found the guns, all hell would break loose—there might even be a war—and there would be no good in having Dee around to talk about how it all began.

Edwards continued his story to the grand jury. Somewhere between the bank and the spot where the youths were picked up, Dee hooked up with Moore, who, as Edwards put it, was purely a victim of circumstance. Now there were two, and James Ford Seale got them both in the car and drove on. In the forest, Seale held a sawed-off shotgun on the boys, warned them against running, and ordered them up against a tree. Edwards and Dunn broke switches as "big as your thumb" from the bushes and administered the "spanking" to the boys while Clyde interrogated them. (The Klan hierarchy of actions against blacks was, from lightest to harshest, spanking, burning, beating, assassination.)

Even though at this point Edwards might not have had the power to save Dee and Moore from their fate—not with Mr. Arch and Mr. Clyde in charge—Fitzgerald wanted Edwards to admit to the grand jury that he knew the certainty of that fate. He waffled: although he might have believed their death was likely, he had no intention of it going that far. Fitzgerald reminded him of his question to Dee—"Are you right with your Lord?"—and he reluctantly admitted he knew both boys were going to "meet their Maker."

Once Dee gave up the location of the guns, Edwards, Mr. Arch, and Mr. Clyde took off to get the law and search the church. When no guns were found, Mr. Clyde, rather than taking Edwards to the farm to help with whatever was going to be done with Moore and Dee, took him home. He told Edwards the others would "take care of the rest of it."

So, was Edwards a villain or a dupe? A perpetrator or a follower? There are no bright lines, but for Fitzgerald's purpose, it's better for Edwards to be a dupe/follower. She has to deal with the fact not only that her star witness has lied consistently for forty-two years about his role in what happened but that he will walk away a free man when the trial is over. It's far better for him to be seen as somewhat of a simpleton who can't quite keep his stories straight rather than a man who willingly sent two black youths to a watery grave and is now scheming to save his own skin.

Edwards, a devout Christian, had a deep and palpable yearning to be forgiven and redeemed. When Fitzgerald finished with her questions, Edwards startled her with a request to address the grand jury. He was welcome to do so, she said. He told the jury a story about rounding a curve as he came home from work one day in 1977 and seeing a house on fire. He stopped, ran up onto the front porch, and banged on the door. Getting no response, he went to the trailer next door and roused the neighbor, who told him there were three children in the house. The two men burst into the burning building. The uncle got the two boys, Edwards grabbed the girl, and everyone made it out just as the house collapsed in flames.

There are three black people—five, if you included the two in the trailer—alive today because of what Edwards did. That should help balance the scales: murder two, save three—and you should be at least even. And, he insisted to the grand jury, he is not a racist: he's got more black friends in Franklin County than anyone who ever lived there. What really irks him about all the civil rights mess is that what he did that day in 1977 was never reported in the *Clarion-Ledger* or any paper in the country. You never heard a word about his saving those black kids' lives. Where's the fairness in that?

The feeling of the unfairness of it all caused Edwards to abandon the high moral ground for a moment, and he took a shot at defending his actions: back then, he insisted, he had done what he thought was right because of the guns and the uprising that was fixing to happen. As if sensing the perilous path he was on, he quickly changed course to one of contrition: "I got involved in something that—that I'm sorry that I ever got involved in. I ask my God every day to forgive me for taking part in this."

The grand jury was in no position to forgive him, but somehow Edwards had seen where possibility lay. Some good might come out of this whole mess; the stain might be washed from his soul; he might one day join his family in heaven.

For Fitzgerald, things had gone well. Her key witness was in a four-point restraint; he couldn't budge an inch. (Or could he?) The not-too-smart, guileless follower, the devout Christian and family man, would play well before a Mississippi jury.

CHAPTER 21

No one seems to know for certain the origin of the rumor about the blacks running guns into Franklin County in 1964. No truth to it was ever found. Edwards told the grand jury that he had come to suspect the whole thing was a hoax spread by the Klan to get the people fired up. (It didn't occur to Edwards to wonder why Clyde Seale would order a search of the church if he knew there were no weapons inside.) With all else that was going on—James Meredith entering Ole Miss, FBI agents and college students from the North invading Mississippi, the integration of the schools—it was not hard for the citizens of Franklin County to accept the truth of the rumor.

Something similar had happened when slavery was the law of the land, and although the citizens might not have heard the specifics of the event, an armed slave uprising was so frightening an image in the South that it might well have existed over the years deep in the cultural mind of this sparsely populated rural county and risen quickly to the surface when rumors of guns and blacks emerged in 1964.

The plan was devised by a white man from Tennessee, John Murrell, who dreamed of setting up an empire in the

Mississippi Valley with Negroes as his army. On July 4, 1836, Negroes on the plantations were to rise up and begin killing their masters with axes, hoes, and clubs while they were drinking and celebrating Independence Day. Negroes would then seize the arms on the plantations and march into town, where they would ransack and burn stores and houses and continue killing whites. When they had recruited enough Negroes, they would attack Natchez, and from Natchez they would spread the terror up and down the land until the entire valley was under control.

The plan was discovered just a few days before the Fourth, when a white man overheard a Negro girl arguing with one of the field hands about the righteousness of killing their master's children. Overseers put Negroes under the whip, and soon the plot unraveled. Hundreds of whites and Negroes were shot or hanged. The Franklin County sheriff killed one of the plot's ringleaders in Meadville.

Although no one was running guns into Franklin County in 1964, and the civil rights movement in the form of sit-ins, boycotts, and marches had not spread here—and in fact never did spread here—some resistance in the black community was beginning. It was led by Pastor Briggs of the First Baptist Church in Roxie, whom, not long before the murders, Constable Jack Davis had witnessed unloading suspiciously larges boxes (which were probably filled with encyclopedias) from his car into the church. It was perhaps this sighting and Briggs's resistance that gave rise to the rumor about the Muslim guns.

CHAPTER 22

Kathy Nester and her private investigator, Mikell Buckley, herself a lawyer and former assistant district attorney, see Edwards as a plain and simple liar. To Buckley, Edwards was just as mean as Seale ever was and totally unremorseful. When they interviewed him in the presence of his lawyers, he talked nigger this and nigger that, a word you never heard from Seale's mouth. Whatever Seale was back then, Buckley believes, he's a changed man now.

During the interview, Edwards totally recanted; he said straight out that Seale had told him nothing about what happened after Dee and Moore were taken from the forest. He had heard nothing, knew nothing. He had only made any statements to the prosecutor because the feds had threatened him and his family. He liked James and felt bad about getting him into this mess. He was not going to testify as to anything that occurred after the forest.

Nester and Buckley left the meeting thinking Edwards might actually be a witness for the defense. Days later, they got a call from his lawyers saying that Edwards had given a written statement implicating Seale but would recant it. According to Nester, during one phone call Graves's associate, Walter Beasley, paused to call Edwards and ask him if he was going to recant. Beasley called Nester back to say that indeed his client would recant. Nester felt confident about her case—without Edwards, the government had nothing.

Since his grand jury testimony, in which he had been very clear about what Seale had said to him, Edwards had apparently begun feeling bad about nailing his friend and was now proposing a distinction he hoped would get him off the hook. As he recalled it now, Seale hadn't told him directly what had happened after the beating in the forest. Seale had been talking to a group of people, not to Edwards in particular. So when he told Nester and Buckley that Seale hadn't told him about what had happened after taking Dee and Moore from the forest, he was telling the truth. However, although Nester and Buckley might have been misled, the lie detector wasn't. When Edwards told the polygraph operator that Seale hadn't told him anything about what happened after the forest, the machine squiggled a lie.

Nester was bitter that the lawyers hadn't told her about the lie detector test at the meeting. She continued to believe that Edwards had recanted, or would do so, until his lawyers finally told her that "the script was written in the grand jury room." Five days before the first hearing in January, she finally received Edwards's statement and realized the duplicity that had been practiced on her and the deep hole her client was now in. She was also angry that the prosecution hadn't polygraphed Edwards's new statement. Once the government got what it wanted—Seale's head—it suddenly believed everything Edwards said.

When Fitzgerald calls out Edwards's name, the courtroom falls instantly still. The turning point is at hand. The chorus and spectators alike understand that the scene about to be played out will tell the tale. People lean forward, as if to focus closely on the door across the room. Minutes pass. Finally, it swings slowly open, and in walks Edwards. He pauses to be sworn in by the clerk, says, "I do," and then turns to the witness stand. You don't necessarily expect a rat to look like a rat—you might not even have an idea of what a rat should look like—but you wonder if there shouldn't be some telltale sign—a little tic, a fluttering eyelid, a raspy voice—to reveal that here is a man who has turned on his comrade, not following a conversion to a different morality or a new God, not out of courage to live with the consequences of past sins, but out of fear, out of knowledge, that he himself will end up in jail unless he sits down in that chair and rats out a friend. You should be able to smell him, this relic of Mississippi's bloody past.

But Edwards, the son of a sharecropper, a hardworking and dedicated family man, couldn't look more innocuous. Dressed in slacks and a short-sleeved white shirt, midsize, stocky but not fat, with a thick mustache and salt-and-pepper hair, his affect, as he is seated and begins answering preliminary questions, is one of simpleminded sincerity, of an honest man who on this day will endeavor to give you the truth as best he can. The only hint of something amiss is his inability to look at James Ford Seale, who sits in dark blue slacks and a light blue shirt, watching his accuser intently. Edwards keeps his eyes on his interrogator, the slender blond woman in the dark suit standing at the podium a few feet in front of him.

Fitzgerald, casually tapping a pen on the podium, proceeds smoothly into the story. She believes her star witness; her task now is to make the jury believe him. He can't appear a complete flunky of the prosecution, saying anything to save his skin, but if he appears too strong, too guilty, the jury might not be able to get over the feeling that it's unfair for him not to pay for the crimes too and wash their hands of the whole affair.

Edwards is a little hard of hearing. A black female clerk leans over and fits a hearing device on his head, brushing his hair slightly. Thelma Collins, Henry Dee's sister, is in the second row with her sisters. Thomas Moore is sitting in the first row with his son. He leans forward and grasps the railing and hangs his head between his arms. Whatever justice is coming to his brother after forty-three years is coming because of the man before him now, who himself uttered the words that set the murders in motion. The jury is quiet.

The spectator rows are almost full. Blacks and movement people have been forced to sit in the rows behind Seale. A group of black summer school students sits on the edge of their seats, witnesses to history. A few local trial lawyers are present to see if Fitzgerald can make Seale into a terrorist from another age who must now be made to pay for his sins and the sins of the time, the sins of Mississippi.

Fitzgerald approaches her witness as a bullfighter might a reluctant bull. She is graceful and elegant, tempting, as she seeks to lure a not-too-smart, and perhaps not-too-brave, animal from the chute and into the ring. She draws the cape slowly across her chest. The bull must come to her, but she must remain in absolute control at all times. She must divert him, not so that he doesn't see the sword sheathed in the cape but so that he forgets that behind the cape is not her but his old comrade in arms, James Ford Seale. He must not swerve off, or the spectators will lose trust.

To establish her adversary's worthiness, Fitzgerald gently leads Edwards through a narrative of who he is and why he's here: He was born in Franklin County, went to school in Meadville, joined the army when he was seventeen, and fought in Korea. He has a wife and four children, one of whom was killed in a hunting accident, and he's been a deacon in his church for forty-two years. He is not here—in the ring—voluntarily. He was forced in front of a grand jury, where it was made clear to him that he must tell the truth or go to jail.

Fitzgerald lowers her cape and sweeps it smoothly in front of her. In 1964 were you a member of the White Knights of the Ku Klux Klan? Yes, he belonged to the Bunkley Klavern. The boss was the defendant's father, Clyde Seale, who swore him in and gave him a copy of the Klan constitution.

Fitzgerald hands Edwards a copy of the constitution and asks him to identify it. Nester stands to object. She fully understands the subtext, and her argument—that the prosecution is trying to put the Klan on trial, that the evidence goes to prove nothing about her client's guilt and is highly prejudicial—is one she has lost repeatedly and is now making for the record. The judge buys Fitzgerald's argument that the oath of secrecy in the constitution is part of the conspiracy, one of the reasons the crime was hidden for forty-three years.

Edwards comes across the field slowly, without further provocation. The Klan was a Christian militant organization, and he was required to prefer the brotherhood over all else. The blacks were the enemy; the Klan's goal was to stop integration of the races wherever the notion raised its ugly head. Yes, violence was an acceptable means to this end. Yes, you could kill, but only if all agreed.

Fitzgerald provokes the witness with a photograph of a man dressed in bright red Klan robes and hat—the same photo flashes on all the courtroom monitors—and he identifies the man as Jack Seale, the defendant's brother (reputed to be the "enforcer" of the Bunkley Klan as well as an FBI informer). The photo serves to bring the flaming images of *Mississippi Burning* more sharply into the charged atmosphere of the courtroom; Jack Seale and his brother James are the same as the men in the movie who burned churches and beat and killed blacks and civil rights workers. Edwards admits to knowing all of the other conspirators, the members of the Bunkley Klan, which was a tight-knit group: Ernest Parker, the owner of the island in the middle of the Mississippi chute, was the only one who didn't live on Bunkley Road.

Steadily but reluctantly, Edwards tells the story of the Klan meeting at which the Muslim guns and insurrection were discussed, and he admits he was the one who gave out Henry Dee's name at the meeting as being a good prospect to help find the guns.

Under Fitzgerald's gentle prodding, Edwards tells the story of how the two boys died that Mississippi spring day. When Clyde and the others came to get him to identify the Dee boy in Meadville, he put down his hoe and got in the back of the truck. He watched Seale pick the boys up.

"James just drove up by them and asked if they wanted a ride. At first they were afraid, but then they piled on in."

He tells how Seale held the sawed-off shotgun on the boys, and he and Curtis Dunn "gave them a spanking" with the switches. After thirty minutes of this, Edwards paused to ask Dee if he was right with the Lord.

"I didn't think he was going to make it."

Fitzgerald leans forward on the podium and asks what that meant.

"They'd be killed," Edwards says.

Fitzgerald goads him on the extent of the beating, and he swivels a little in his path, responding tautly that he doesn't know how many times the boys were struck and doesn't remember seeing any blood. Yes, he helped with the search of the church, and then he was taken home. At a Klan meeting that night, Mr. Clyde told him things were "taken care of." He knew what that meant.

Now, the moment of truth. Fitzgerald must keep Edwards coming steadily at her; he must not see that his path leads to the frail body of his former fellow Klansman. Eyes front, eyes on her. The slightest hesitation and the finish will be messy. She holds him in her gaze. What happened after the forest?

Edwards testifies that he was talking with Mr. Clyde, Mr. Arch, Jack Seale, and James Seale, when James began telling the story of how he and Dunn loaded the boys up in his car and took them to Mr. Clyde's farm. There, James taped their mouths and hands, and the boys were tossed in the trunk of Ernest Parker's car. The car was driven through Natchez, across the bridge into Louisiana, and north to Parker's Island.

Fitzgerald calls to her witness across the distance—What happened next, Mr. Edwards?—and pulls the cape away to reveal the body of the alleged murderer, waiting helplessly for the blows. Edwards veers slightly toward his target and charges straight into him: Seale said that he and two others weighted Dee with an engine block, tied chains around him, put him in a boat, and rowed out into the river, where they pushed him overboard. The image Fitzgerald painted in her opening statement of Charles Moore watching the death of his friend and waiting for his turn to die comes rushing back into the courtroom. Seale and another man then took Moore, now chained to rails, to the boat to join his friend in a muddy Mississippi grave. Edwards pulls up hard: the youths were in the forest when he last saw them. Alive.

Fitzgerald eyes him sternly for a moment, as if to impress this truth in the minds of the jury, and returns to her seat. She is in good shape. Edwards did well; he bumbled a little, but not too much. He is not clever or deceptive. He is a simple man, a flawed man, who had only lied to protect his family.

CHAPTER 23

Kathy Nester walks slowly to the podium and looks calmly at her quarry for a few seconds. Her job is to finish Edwards off in such a way as to make the jury forget the goring it has just witnessed. Her client, who watched Edwards coming at him with pale eyes and took the blow without flinching, is nonetheless battered and bleeding. She must strike quickly before the image crystallizes. She goes straight at Edwards, not sure how wary or deft he might be at this stage of the fight, convinced only that he is a liar and a far worse man than her client.

Nester has in mind for Edwards a death by a thousand cuts, a thousand pics in the key muscles, until his head drops, and he stumbles to the ground. He does not look at her as he agrees one by one to the many lies he has told—to the FBI agents, time and again, to the prosecutors, time and again, to Connie Chung, to the defense lawyers themselves. Each time he admits to a lie, Nester writes "lie" with a flourish on a tablet sitting on a large easel. When first arrested in 1964 for the murders, Edwards denied that he was in the Klan—"lie"; he denied then that he knew everything about what had happened to the boys after the forest—"lie"; he told Connie Chung he knew nothing of the murder—"lie"; and he told her he knew nothing of the Klan—"lie." On and on. He remains un-ruffled as she runs through his endless lies, until she confronts him with his 1964 confession to beating the boys in the forest, which he continues to deny making. Edwards's face reddens; a blustery anger surfaces.

"If I confessed, why wasn't I arrested?" he demands.

"Good question," Nester deadpans.

Edwards is done passively taking the pics; he's turning on Nester, playing into her hands. One waits to see if she can draw him into a wild lunge, one that will leave him open and exposed. When Nester mentions that in the 1964 confession he had said they beat the boys because they had been peeping at his wife, he stiffens. A shock of violence flares in his eyes. If those boys had bothered his wife, he insists, they would never have been found in the river. Does he mean that he would have drowned them in deeper water so they would never have floated to the surface or that he would have hung them instead? All because they had peeped through a window at his wife.

For an instant, the southern white man's greatest fear—that his women will be subject to the sexual predations of a black man—has gripped him. In a woman's purity lies a man's honor, and honor is worth killing, or getting killed, for. To even think of a black man peeping through a window at his wife is to besmirch her—and therefore him—forever, so the notion cannot have come from him; even the suggestion of the act from Nester's mouth is infuriating, humiliating.

Nester moves on to another of the southerners' biggest fears in those days. Didn't he say something about the

"Communists" to the agents? Edwards stares warily at her. Yes, he did tell the agents in '64 that rather than bothering him, they should be in Selma rounding up the commies. The aggrieved tone in his voice says he still believes that's what the agents should have been doing.

He tells the jury that he was the son of a sharecropper. He worked right along with the blacks in the fields as a boy.

"I am not a racist," he declaims indignantly. "From the bottom of my heart, I'm telling you the truth."

Nester jabs deeply, hoping to get another charge out of him, a clumsy stupid charge that will drop him.

"Isn't that what you told *ABC News*? That you were telling the truth from the bottom of your heart?"

Edwards calms down. "Yes, ma'am," he says solemnly.

Nester pics again. Well, why did you keep silent for all these years? He picks up the Klan constitution and waves it in the air indignantly, dramatically, as if she should know the very answer: He swore an oath of secrecy! He was trying to protect James!

Ah, he was lying all those years to protect a friend, but now he's telling the truth to screw the same friend. He was lying all these years in obedience to an oath sworn to a murdering racist organization, but he was never a racist.

Nester withdraws the pic, letting the blood trickle slowly from the wound. "Why did you finally tell the truth then?" she asks, modulating the contempt in her voice. When he failed the polygraph test, the agent threatened to bring his family into the case and told him that he could also go to jail. This notion seems to stabilize Edwards: he was willing to go to jail to protect Seale, but family comes first. Family is sacred. Edwards drums the rail with his fingers.

Nester looks at him steadily. The story. Tell us the story James Ford Seale told you. Exactly what he told you he did to those boys that day. Edwards falls back on his old distinction: Seale didn't actually tell him anything; there was a group—the old gang, really, including Mr. Clyde, Mr. Arch, and James himself—and it was a round-robin sort of discussion, a conversation, more or less, but James did most of the talking. Although Edwards doesn't know when the conversation took place, he has a quite sharp recollection of the details, like Seale describing the route the killers drove from the farm to Parker's Island and how they rolled the boys overboard alive.

The picture is of a marginal Edwards hanging on the edge of the group of men, eavesdropping almost as, for whatever reason, they recounted the details of that bloody event. Someday, one of them surely would have told Edwards what happened, if for no other reason than to remind him of his own culpability and the need to keep his mouth shut, but why would all of the details come out of James Seale's mouth in the presence of two of the other killers? He was a braggart, to be sure, but would he brag in front of the two big dogs, Mr. Clyde and Mr. Arch? If the conversation happened, the three men were probably reliving the day, perhaps to thin out their individual guilt by spreading it around or to jack themselves up as to why the deed had to be done. Maybe they were talking it over to get their stories straight. It couldn't have been James Seale laying out the facts of the day and his role in them in some weird confessional monologue. Maybe in Edwards's mind the story now streams only from the mouth of Seale, or maybe it's just an easier story to tell that way. If Edwards had gotten into who actually said what—James said this, and Mr. Clyde said that, and Mr. Arch went on about this—the fragile cloth of his story could easily have come unraveled.

Nester has two problems with Edwards: Why would he lie and where would he learn the facts of the lie? That is, how would he know what lie to make up? The answer to the first question is just a slight spin on Edwards's explanation for telling the truth. Edwards claims he told the truth to save his family; Nester says he made up the lie to satisfy the prosecution, to give them what they wanted so they would leave him and his family alone. Not particularly convincing, but it's all she's got.

The second problem is a bit trickier, and the path to the answer lies over highly treacherous ground for the defense. Nester wants to prove that everything Edwards has said he could have learned from some source other than her client. The problem is, the only other source for the facts of the story is Ernest Gilbert. But if Gilbert's name comes up, the jury might want to know a little more about him and exactly what it was he said. And then the door might swing open for the much-feared Gilbert statement to come into evidence.

Early in the cross-examination, Nester stumbles across the land mine. She asks Edwards where he had heard that James Seale was worried about his fingerprints being on the duct tape he placed over the boys' mouths.

"From the FBI reports," he replies.

"What FBI reports?"

"I guess those reports that came from Ernest Gilbert."

She moves on. Fitzgerald, watching intently, says nothing. Toward the end of her cross, Nester asks Edwards if he would agree with her that every fact he'd testified to had been covered in the media.

EDWARDS: Yes, ma'am. I do. Ernest Gilbert, that informant the FBI had—
NESTER: Wait. I need to stop you right there. That is not proper to talk about that right now.
EDWARDS: Well, that's where it came from.
NESTER: So you—let's talk about it, then, without using names.

It is too late: Gilbert's name has now been put out on the board, not once but twice. Still, Fitzgerald remains quiet. Only when Nester has finished her cross-examination and returned to her seat does she strike.

Your honor, she insists, rising from her chair and moving swiftly to the podium, dark eyes alive with indignation, Ms. Nester has now opened the door on Gilbert's statement. The jury has heard it referred to twice by Edwards as a source of his information about what happened after Moore and Dee were taken from the forest. The jury is entitled to see for themselves if everything Edwards said was indeed contained in Gilbert's statement. The jurors must be allowed to read Gilbert's statement for themselves and check the items off. Otherwise, they will be left with the undisputed impression that Edwards knew nothing that wasn't in Gilbert's statement.

Nothing has happened so far in the trial to change Nester's view that her client is a dead man if the statement comes in. It will show that he shot his mouth off twice about his deed, both times to fellow Klansmen, telling essentially the same story each time. She has fought hard to keep it out, and the judge, perhaps realizing that the door has in fact been opened but knowing the trial will essentially be over if he lets it in, recesses for a transcript to be prepared and for counsel to brief the issue.

After the jury is excused, Edwards doesn't rise immediately from his chair. Glancing up at Judge Wingate, he says, "I want to speak to the families of Mr. Moore and Mr. Dee." Before the judge can respond, Edwards leans forward in his chair and looks directly at Thomas Moore seated across the room.

"I can't undo what was done forty years ago, and I'm sorry for that. And I ask your forgiveness for my part in that crime. That's exactly what I wanted to say to you."

Moore, as if knowing what is coming, looks over at the wall as Edwards begins speaking. At the last few words, he turns and looks Edwards in the eye.

In a simple, brilliant stroke, the religious factory worker and family man has turned his moment of infamy into an opportunity for redemption. You can't gain redemption with just an admission of guilt; you must seek the forgiveness of those whom you have harmed. And he has done just that.

Jeannie watches her husband walk unsteadily from the courtroom and thinks of all the cruel things others say he has done. If she could only get on the stand herself and tell the jury of the James she knows. About the day when they were standing in a courthouse in a small Alabama town during a terrible rainstorm, and a black prisoner on grounds duty came in soaked and freezing. James took his jacket off, gave it to the man, and never saw it again.

Or about the time when she and James visited her mother in a nursing home in Alabama and found her in bed in badly soiled nightclothes. James took his boots off, gently picked her up, and carried her into the shower, where he held her under the warm water and washed her clean. He might not be an angel, but he didn't kill those boys. James wanted to take the stand and tell his own story, but his attorneys wouldn't let him. It will be over soon, she thinks, and he will be coming home.

Chapter 24

Judge Wingate glances curiously down at Edwards. In courts of law, the role of the witness is simply to answer questions. Some judges, particularly federal judges, would view such behavior from a witness—addressing members of the audience from the stand—as an affront to the dignity of the court. But the judge says nothing. Edwards steps down from the dais and walks slowly to the door. "All rise!" the clerk calls, the judge exits through a door behind the bench, and the curtain clangs shut.

Thelma Collins, Henry Dee's sister, sits still in the courtroom for a few moments and lets Edwards's statement sink in. She has no hate in her heart about her brother's death. She believes it took courage for Edwards to turn to the family, say he was sorry, and ask for forgiveness.

When Thelma Collins and Thomas Moore leave the courthouse, reporters gather around on the steps and insist on a response to Edwards's request. Thelma speaks her mind—"I think he's a good man who got caught up in the wrong thing"—and the newspeople scurry off into the wet heat with their quote.

Across the street, the state flag in front of the governor's mansion hangs limp in the windless air, obscuring the Stars and Bars. Downtown Jackson seems so remote from the tragedy being played out in the courtroom. It seems a thriving metropolis: the streets are clean and well land-scaped, the stores are all occupied, office buildings are a mix of old and new, well-dressed black and white busi-nessmen and -women stream down the street, and the hammering and clanging of new construction sound constantly.

Jackson is the best of the South. The blues clubs in the area feel authentic; their acts are not imported from Chicago and Memphis but come from Hattiesburg and Clarksdale and Tupelo. At Hal and Mal's, a legendary club not far from the courthouse—nothing is far away in Jackson—the musicians, young and old, black and white, mix and hang out with each other and the patrons like it's all one family, and when they sing and play, their stories feel intertwined, as if they'd sprung from the same root. Nothing has to be explained; it's all understood.

On the other hand, Jackson is now supposedly one of the most dangerous cities in the country. An FBI report shows that between 2005 and 2006 the city incurred a 42 percent increase in violent crime. Jackson came in ahead of Memphis, Detroit, and Los Angeles in murders per capita and ranked eighth in rapes. Areas of the west side of Jack-son are the scene of heavy drug use and trafficking and all the violence that goes with it. Plans to invest in the Farish Street area of town hang in the balance, caught in the vi-cious politics of a black mayor, majority-black city council, white governor, and white-controlled state legislature.

Charges of corruption and malfeasance at all levels of city government are commonplace. Lawyers are tried and convicted of bribing judges. Some black activists accuse the mayor, reviled by many liberal whites, of being a stooge for white business interests.

But the city doesn't feel dangerous; it feels, at least in some areas, quite urbanely civilized. In the northern part of town, close to Millsaps College, a renowned liberal arts school, is writer and poet Eudora Welty's elegantly maintained home and garden, where genteel southern ladies are delighted to take a visitor on an extended tour of the house and the grounds. A little further north is a first-class university medical facility and a small Bohemian district.

Little things tell you you're not in a northern capital city. You seldom get a parking ticket; if you do and neglect to pay it, nothing happens. If you mention to the owner of a downtown deli that that you like the music playing, he might burn you a CD on the spot. If you approach someone for directions, the person is likely to walk you to your destination. If you're a dollar short, you can pay next time. There is no rush hour in Jackson. The cathedral across from the state capitol is Baptist, not Catholic.

But the play is still the thing. The Edison Walthall Hotel sits in the middle of the block west of the federal courthouse. The government has housed all of its witnesses here, under the care of former FBI agent Jim Ingram. After Edwards's apology in court, he told Ingram that he had done what he had to do and felt good for it. The next day, in the hotel hallway, he ran into Thelma Collins and Thomas Moore. Edwards told them again how sorry he was for what he'd done. Moore replied simply that he forgave him. Collins, in tears, said she forgave him as well. Edwards thanked them. "It's a great load off my conscience," he said. "I know I will have to live with it the rest of my life."

James Ford Seale at the time of his arrest in 1964
for the murders of Charles Moore and Henry Dee.

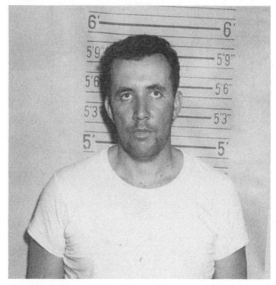

Charles Marcus Edwards at the time of his arrest
in 1964 for the murders of Charles Moore and
Henry Dee.

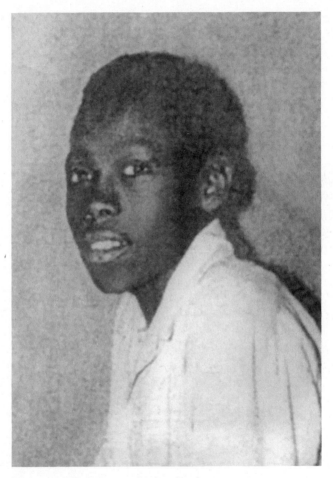

Henry Ezekiah Dee in high school.

Charles Eddie Moore in high school.

Thomas Moore, older brother of Charles Moore, in 2007.
He was determined to find justice for Charles and Henry.

James Ford Seale in 2007
being led to federal court
in a bulletproof vest.

Charles Marcus Edwards
at the trial of James Ford
Seale in 2007.

Emmett Till, the boy from Chicago whose murder is often credited with sparking the civil rights movement.

CHAPTER 25

Forgiveness. Atonement. Redemption. Reconciliation. Of all these terms wound up so intimately in Mississippi's effort at cultural and moral reconstruction, the last is the most elusive. Perhaps it's like Supreme Court Justice Potter Stewart said of pornography: you know it when you see it. With reconciliation, you know it when you feel it.

When you stick "racial" in front of the word "reconciliation," the term becomes even less certain and more charged. It surely means, in the South, equality before God and the law. But does it go to what's in the individual's heart? Does it mean blacks and whites have to respect one another? Love one another? Or is it enough to acknowledge each other's differences and strive for economic and social justice, for fundamental fairness in all aspects of living? Hoping that even though the past might never die, perhaps the heart, with the passing of time and generations, will eventually come around.

Perhaps there is no definition of racial reconciliation because there's no example of it, at least no contemporary example of it after the institution of slavery. An enslaved race might come to terms with its former oppressors, live side by side, but it's an uncertain path beyond that point. Racial reconciliation seems to be a term waiting to be defined. James Meredith, who integrated Ole Miss and today greets visitors to his Jackson home in an Ole Miss cap, sees a great opportunity for his home state. Mississippi has the highest ratio of blacks to whites of any state in the nation, and the two races live and work together every day. He believes that whites here fear blacks less than whites in any other state. They know each other better than anywhere in the world. Mississippi could lead the way—and maybe Ole Miss could lead Mississippi.

Many symbols of the Old South are wound into the traditions of the University of Mississippi, the nurturing bosom of the ruling white aristocracy since the school's founding in 1848. A few symbols, like the name "Ole Miss," which was the slave name for the mistress of the plantation, have been allowed to transform gradually into modern traditions. Others, like displaying the Confederate flag or playing "Dixie" at Ole Miss football games, as well as the mascot Colonel Reb, have been controversial for years and to this day remain irritants for some.

At Ole Miss, symbols exist in a strange confusion with the present. A young Confederate soldier, left hand raised to shade his eyes, stands erect and proud atop a marble column at the entrance to the fabled Grove, ten acres of land shaded by oak, elm, and magnolia trees in the center of campus. Less than one hundred yards away stands the statue of James Meredith in coat and tie passing through Greek columns on his way to register at Ole Miss. The William Winter Institute for Racial Reconciliation is housed in Vardaman Hall, named after perhaps the most virulently racist governor in Mississippi's history. The Lyceum, a three-story Greek Revival building named after the garden where Aristotle taught and the visual symbol of the university, was used as a hospital for wounded Confederate soldiers after the battles of Shiloh and Corinth during the Civil War. Federal marshals surrounded the Lyceum during the 1962 riots over Meredith's admission, and the administration has carefully preserved the bullet holes in the walls. Black students sit in classrooms in a campus building in which is preserved a stained glass window depicting the University Grays, students and professors at Ole Miss who enlisted and fought in the Confederate army, a great many of whom died in Pickett's Charge at Gettysburg. Blacks and whites live in separate houses on fraternity row. (The campus is about 50 percent Greek.) Social gatherings, including lunchroom seating, concerts, and parties are self-segregated, although student groups (such as One Mississippi) have sprung up in recent years to challenge this practice. Two recent student-body presidents have been black; two white candidates for the current position, both Republicans, ran on platforms of racial reconciliation. This supposed bastion of the decadent Old South was recently ranked among the top twenty-five public universities by *Forbes Magazine*.

Oxford is only a short distance from campus and lies on the Trail of Tears, the path by which several Indian tribes, including the Chickasaw, Choctaw, and Cherokee, were removed from their ancestral lands and marched west to Oklahoma. William Faulkner lived a few blocks from the Oxford town square on a large estate he named Rowan Oak. A bronze figure of the author sitting comfortably on a bench and smoking a pipe rests in front of the town hall, which was burned down, along with the county courthouse across the street, by Union troops in 1864. In front of the current courthouse stands another statute of a Confederate soldier holding a long rifle. Inscribed on the base are the words, "They gave their lives in a just and holy cause."

Faulkner, whose grandfather served as a colonel in the Confederate army, opposed segregation, but he also opposed forced integration on the grounds that whites wouldn't allow it and the blacks weren't ready for it. At the time he wrote *The Sound and the Fury*, 43 percent of the state's population could not attend the state university a few miles from where he lived. Today, a visitor to Ole Miss or Oxford would be hard pressed to find a vehicle flying anything resembling the Stars and Bars, yet very few black students hang around the square, patronizing the restaurants or bookstores. Fewer still attend the tailgating parties at the Grove.

Some black students might be coming to Ole Miss these days with the goal of further integrating the school or challenging the existing order. But many are now coming to get the first-rate education they are entitled to as citizens of Mississippi. One black student recalls how his parents were shocked when he told them he wanted to attend Ole Miss. Finally reconciled to the idea, his grandmother sat him down and told him to work hard at the university so he could advance himself and be equal with whites. He tried to explain to her that he wasn't going to college to be equal with whites or change things; he was going to Ole Miss to get a good education so he could do what he chose with his life.

CHAPTER 26

Reconciliation at Ole Miss is one thing; it is quite another in the real world of the Delta. As the people in Sumner found out, the path toward reconciliation in a land with this terrible history is unpredictable and perilous. The original makeup of the Emmett Till Commission was six blacks and three whites. A black served as chair. For the first few meetings in 2006, only black members showed up and the few people in the audience were black. County Supervisor Jerome Little knew that the whites on the commission had to be people with power and respect. He made sure that Betty Pearson was one of them, and when he approached her in the spring of that year to ask why she hadn't attended the meetings, she said, "Why, Jerome, what on earth are you talking about? No one's told me a thing." Turned out, the other two whites on the board hadn't been notified either. Heads shook, but no one could figure out what had happened.

The Emmett Till Commission meetings were held in a conference room on the second floor of the courthouse. In the beginning, it was awkward for everyone. Jerome Little and Bobby Banks, another black supervisor, could

not, despite Pearson's pleas, address her as anything but
"Mrs. Pearson." Her threat to stop addressing them as
"Bobby" and "Jerome," as she had done for years, had no
effect. "We just couldn't [call you Betty]," they insisted.
"We just couldn't."

Little and Banks had no illusions about white people.
Blacks in Sumner had fought for everything they had.
Blacks had had to sue the county over inadequate sewer
systems and schools and a lack of black elected officials.
Whites always had an agenda. They wanted to control
everything and give up as little as possible.

"I'll be frank with you," Little said at one of the early
commission meetings. "I'm afraid of whites because what
you're going to do on the commission is take it over. You
always want to be in charge of everything."

Pearson listened calmly, then, in her best direct but
nonconfrontational manner, replied, "You're probably
right, Jerome. Frank [Mitchener] and I like to be in charge
of things; that is something you probably better worry
about. But there are black people on this board who want
to be in control too, so it's not totally a white thing. It's
something we need to be aware of and look at."

Whites of Sumner didn't want to be co-opted into a
black event bent on pillorying the white community. They
could never quite get over the fact that the murderers
weren't from their town, and the crimes hadn't been
committed there. And what was the point in dredging up
the past?

Pearson explained the situation to the white community at a town meeting called to discuss the project: the
reality is that the Till trial took place in this courthouse,

whether the boy was killed here or not and whether the defendants were from here or not. The trial has historical importance, not only for Mississippi but for the country, and it is wrong for Sumner to be defensive about it, as if it were something to be ashamed of. What we should be saying is, yes, this historical event happened here, but the town is not that way now. Accept the crime as part of your past, but look forward in a positive way.

Pearson didn't mention the term "racial reconciliation" at the meeting; nor did she say outright that the commission's effort was the best, if not the only, path to the restoration of the courthouse. But the message was there. The town was slowly fading: Emmett Till, the martyr, could be the community's salvation.

Little was getting heat from blacks. Some felt that the whites were out to take advantage of Emmett Till, that they were only truly interested in the restoration of the courthouse. One black minister stood up at a meeting and raised hell: the whole thing was going to be a white show; the town was going to use a brutally murdered black boy to fix the courthouse and have tourists come and look at it. The project was a desecration of Emmett Till's memory. The minister demanded to know what was in it for the black community. Little and Banks had sold out to the whites.

But even as tensions rose among the people of Sumner, Pearson and Little both instinctively understood that although the interests of the blacks and whites might be different, they were not competing. The key to getting where they wanted lay in developing trust. So the commission members talked and talked. The meetings were only supposed to last an hour, but they dragged on into the evening. Often no action was taken. Mitchener, in his mid-seventies, white haired, handsome and opinionated, maintained a businessman's attitude, and he stood up and left the room at the appointed hour. The others stayed and talked, perhaps each still getting used to the sight of the other across the table. And they talked some more.

Little got in touch with Susan Glisson, the woman who had helped form the Philadelphia Coalition, the group of citizens in Neshoba County largely responsible for bringing pressure to bear on the authorities to reopen the case on the murder of the three civil rights workers. Glisson agreed to help. She soon brought a needed process to the meetings, always careful only to facilitate, not to direct or manage. She held up the coalition model as a way to begin the discussion.

Glisson raised the issue of the commission's racial makeup: six blacks and three whites. Not good. The whole thing could look like a sop to the black community, which the white community could then easily dismiss. The Philadelphia Coalition had been very careful to balance its board racially between whites, blacks, and Choctaws. Little saw the implications: if you were in the minority, it would be damn easy to walk out over an issue, and the whites must be kept at the table at all costs.

The commission was soon expanded to eighteen members, nine white and nine black, with black and white cochairs. Betty Pearson was elected the white cochair, and Mayor Robert Grayson of Tutwiller, who had grown up picking cotton on Pearson's father's plantation, was elected the black cochair. The commission, now committed to racial balance and diversity, struggled with how to account for the Chinese, of which there are many in the Delta. After much discussion, the commission decided to consider them as white, thereby not requiring separate representation. (The racial status of Chinese in Mississippi has always been in dispute. In 1909 the Mississippi Supreme Court declared Chinese to be "colored" so as to prevent their admittance to white schools. In 1927 the U.S. Supreme Court in *Gong Lum v. Rice* held, in effect, that classifying those of the "yellow races" as colored did not violate the equal protection clause of the Fourteenth Amendment. In the forties and fifties, the status of the Chinese in the Delta gradually shifted to white.)

The commission continued talking and negotiating, but it also began mobilizing. With the help of a local lawyer, it adopted a set of bylaws. Glisson drafted and faxed agendas and minutes, and she followed up with notes and phone calls. She provided protocol and stability, while gently moving the commission in what she believed to be the right direction.

Emmett Till had, metaphorically speaking, risen from the dead only a few years earlier. His murder and the trial of his killers did not loom large in the last half of the twentieth century. The fiftieth anniversary of his death in 2005 brought his story to life. Books and articles were written, plays produced, and songs sung. Mississippi woke up to the fact that, in spite of its successful prosecutions of other old race crimes, no serious effort to find and prosecute Emmett Till's murderers had been made since the acquittals of J. W. Milam and Roy Bryant fifty years earlier.

On May 10, 2004, in a remarkable conjoining of local law enforcement and the federal government, the Justice Department and the district attorney for Sunflower, Leflore, and Washington counties announced a joint investigation into Till's murder. Since the federal government had no jurisdiction of the crime, it was agreed that the FBI would conduct the investigation and present the evidence to a state grand jury. Although a documentary entitled *The Untold Story of Emmett Till*, produced by Mississippi native Keith Beauchamp, claimed that fourteen men had been involved in the crime, four of them black, and that five of them were still alive, the unspoken target of the investigation was Carolyn Bryant. The word had always been that a female voice had been heard at the scene of the kidnapping identifying Till as the boy who had allegedly accosted Bryant in the store and whistled at her when she came outside. A manslaughter charge was seen as a possibility.

In May 2005, Chicago city officials exhumed Emmett Till's body from the cemetery where it had lain for fifty years. The Cook County coroner performed the first autopsy on the body. It was positively identified using dental records as that of Emmett Till, and the cause of death was ruled a homicide: a bullet to the head. He also had fractures to the skull and legs and broken wrist bones. There was no evidence to support the rumors that he had been castrated and holes drilled in his skull.

Back in Sumner, Jerome Little kept careful watch on the work of the FBI and the grand jury, which was run by black district attorney Joyce Chiles. He had hopes that he could tie the commission's event in Sumner to the announcement of a grand jury indictment, or even to an announcement that there would be no indictment. Either version would bring the national spotlight to the community and the commission.

Racial reconciliation on the commission continued to be a delicate and unpredictable process. Little's job was to keep the blacks at the table; Pearson's job was to keep the whites there. Over the months, there were tears and shouting scenes and brooding silences. More than once, the whites huddled in one corner of the room and the blacks in the other. The challenge was keeping the members in the present while dealing with the past, coping with feelings of resentment and guilt in a way that was honest but not destructive, that allowed movement into the future without loss of dignity on either side.

Little got fired up. With Glisson at his side, he traveled to Neshoba County and met with the Philadelphia Coalition. He listened to stories of how the coalition had coped with racial stress. He heard about the apology Secretary of State Richard Molpus issued in 1989 at a memorial service commemorating the twenty-fifth anniversary of the deaths and about the apology the coalition issued in a May 2004 statement. A vital piece of the puzzle snapped into place: the apology would be the centerpiece of the memorial celebration. He would demand an apology from Governor Barbour, the U.S. attorney general, and even from President Bush. It would transform the day into a truly national event.

Little examined a coalition driving tour brochure containing a map, photos, and a discussion of all the sites involved in the Neshoba County murders. The commission decided that it would also prepare a brochure and erect historical markers at each of the sites, such as Bryant's grocery, the cotton gin, the spot in the river where the body was found, and the dilapidated funeral parlor where Emmett Till's body was embalmed.

The commission believed that the project could help gather tourism dollars for the impoverished county. The Emmett Till Museum would be built across the street from the courthouse. Volunteers would hand out brochures and conduct bus tours of the sites.

Little let the racial genie out of the bottle at one meeting. He suggested that the commission invite Jesse Jackson or Al Sharpton to the ceremony. An uproar ensued. One white woman challenged Little on why they needed Jackson or Sharpton for the event; couldn't their community speak for itself? Another white woman became hysterical at the very notion of either of these men coming to Sumner—she would resign from the commission first! In tears, the woman got up from the table and left the room. Over the next few days, Betty Pearson reassured her that the men would not be invited and gradually convinced her to come back to the table. The topic was not brought up again, although Little nourished a flicker of resentment that he couldn't say what he wanted without whites threatening to leave the table.

Pearson scored another victory. The commission's new treasurer was a black minister and auto repair shop owner by the name of Willie Williams, whom she had known for years. She asked him one day, "Willie, do you think you could find it within you to call me Betty?"

He replied, "No ma'am. I can't do that."

"Now, Willie," she said, "just think about it: we're trying to be friends, trying to get some things done as equals in the community, and if you insist on calling me Mrs. Pearson, and I call you Willie, we're perpetuating the old plantation mentality. There are plenty of white guys younger than you who call me Betty."

"I see what you mean," Willie replied. "Sure, I can call you Betty."

At the next commission meeting, Willie addressed Pearson as Betty. Heads, black and white, snapped up around the table. Who did he think he was?

Little's dream of coordinating the commemoration in Sumner with the announcement of the grand jury's indictments in the murder of Till would not come to pass. In February 2007 the grand jury disbanded without action. It appeared that no one directly involved in the crime was still alive—at least no one who would talk. Perhaps worse for the commission's future, a serious schism was brewing between some of the whites and blacks. It arose over the use of one word in the proposed proclamation to be issued by the commission at the ceremony; apology.

Chapter 27

When the court reconvenes, the defense and prosecution undertake once again to convince Judge Wingate of the correctness of their positions on the admissibility of Gilbert's damning statement. Seale, seemingly even thinner, watches the arguments back and forth with grim passivity. Wingate eventually decides not to decide, to take the matter under consideration. The prosecution will call additional witnesses, and he will rule later, when he has made up his mind.

The story of what became of the two teenagers has not yet been fully told. The jury knows that the bottom halves of their bodies were recovered on July 13 and 14, but they know nothing of the discoveries in the fall. Particularly in murder cases, the defense usually attempts to prevent the admission of the grisly evidence of the crime by offering to simply agree that the deceased died in a certain manner at a certain time in a certain way. But courts long ago decided that the prosecution can't be forced to stipulate away its case. The government is entitled to tell and show the gory story of the crime in reasonable detail, the only limitation being that the evidence can't be unduly inflammatory, whatever that means exactly. Here, the court has already ruled that photos of the remains will be shown to the jury.

Retired navy diver Richard Bladh, an elderly, slender, dignified man with white hair and mustache and wearing a pressed blue suit, steps shakily to the stand. After settling in, he corrects prosecutor Eric Gibson that he is in fact eighty-one, not seventy-one, which causes a ripple of laughter through the courtroom. For the next few minutes, he relives the story of his role in the morality play with great clarity and firm detail, as if feeling the pride once again of being a navy diver.

In October 1964 he had been sent to Mississippi for a "body job." The first day, the FBI directed his team well upriver from where the remains were thought to be, to protect an informant, he was told. The divers conducted a line search; one diver sat in an anchored boat while another, holding a rope, swam in a circle in the swirling water and felt blindly along the muddy bottom. The circle was buoyed, and the rope was lengthened, and the diver went out again. For three days the divers found nothing but clutter. On the fourth day, they moved to the hot area, 150 feet from the bank, and they soon uncovered two pieces of railroad track and two rollers connected by logging chains. Bladh himself found rib bones entangled in a shirt and brought them to the surface.

The next day, the divers came across an engine block, chains, and more bones. At midday, a diver surfaced and pointed to his head, indicating he had found a skull. The diver brought to the surface a shiny black skull. Bladh was startled; in all his dives for human remains, he had never seen a black skull. He figured the action of the Mississippi mud must have polished it.

A photograph flashes on the screens around the court-room. A black skull sits on the planks of a white dock between an engine block, chains, and rails. It's Charles Moore. Nub, nineteen years old, missing his four front teeth.

Bladh explains that the search was called off soon after the discovery of Moore's skull. Dee's skull was never recovered.

Thelma Collins is absent, but Thomas Moore and his son are in their regular places. During the testimony, spectators glance from the skull to Moore to see how he's reacting. He stares flatly into the space just beyond the monitor. At the break, reporters cluster around him—"Hard day, Thomas?" they ask in solemn tones—but Thomas, who's seen the photos before, shakes his head. "Not too bad."

CHAPTER 28

In 1964 the FBI and most locals believed Franklin County sheriff Wayne Hutto and Patrolman Bernice Beasley to be members of the Mississippi White Knights of the Ku Klux Klan. (Hutto was named as an unindicted coconspirator in the indictment brought against Seale in 2007.) On the morning of May 2, 1964, the two lawmen were in the Franklin County Courthouse in Meadville when Clyde Seale, Archie Prather, and Charles Edwards walked in and announced there were guns in the colored Baptist church in Roxie. The men wanted the lawmen to get a warrant and search the place.

Hutto and Beasley most likely inquired of their fellow Klansmen as to the source of their information—"Where'd you boys learn that?"—if one of the three hadn't volunteered it first. The three Klansmen, flush with the excitement of the beating and wired by the possibility of finding Muslim guns in a colored church, surely recounted to the sheriff and patrolman what they had done in the woods and to whom. With or without a warrant—one was never found—the lawmen wouldn't have rushed off to search the church without something solid to go on. Which meant that the two lawmen were complicit in the kidnapping and eventual murder of Dee and Moore.

The group of men found the church locked. They located Pastor Briggs at the home of a friend in Crosby, a town not far from Roxie. They told Briggs they heard the church had guns in it and that it was going to be bombed that night. Briggs followed the officers to Roxie in his car and unlocked the building. The lawmen searched the entire church, even tore up the floor boards and got into the attic, but found no guns.

In 1964 the FBI questioned both Hutto and Beasley repeatedly about the murders. Both denied knowing anything about Moore and Dee. Neither man told the FBI about the search of the church, undoubtedly aware that to do so would have inevitably led back to Dee and Moore and their own involvement in their deaths. (One of the first questions from the FBI would have been, why did you search the church that morning?) It had been in the lawmen's power to interrupt the events that led to the murder of Henry Dee and Charles Moore that morning.

Local law enforcement's connection to the murders went undiscovered for forty-two years. In an article on the murders in 2005, the *Jackson Free Press* wrote that during the beating in the forest either Dee or Moore had given the Klansman the name of a preacher. John Briggs, son of Clyde Briggs, recognized the preacher as his father, contacted the paper, and soon began working with the U.S. Attorney. In a meeting with Dunn Lampton, Briggs suddenly remembered that his father had kept a journal in the sixties. John found the journal in the attic, and turned it over to Lampton. The journal contained a description of the search of the First Baptist Church on May 2, 1964, the day of the murders.

The journal was a huge find for the prosecution because it corroborated Edwards's story about the search and therefore Edwards's entire story. Gilbert never mentioned a search of the church, but Edwards detailed it in his own statement. The search for the Muslim guns was a crucial fact that only Edwards knew.

On the stand, John Briggs and his sister Chastity identify the handwriting in the journal as that of their father. John raises eyebrows by claiming that he believes the FBI and the Klan poisoned his father in 1965, but Chastity counters that her father died of pneumonia. Chastity, who attended college with Charles Moore, verifies sections in the journal that tell stories of Klan harassment of her father.

The wife and daughter of Vernon Dahmer, the civil rights leader killed by the Klan in Hattiesburg in 1966, observe the day's testimony from the first row of benches. "Thank God the Mississippi of today is not the Mississippi of the past," his daughter, Bettie, remarks to a reporter during a break. Ellie, his wife, comments that "Sam Bowers once said he would never go to jail for killing a nigger. Well, Sam Bowers died in prison for killing a nigger." The feeling among the movement people in the courtroom is that James Seale is another Sam Bowers and that he should die in jail as well.

Seale smiles at his wife as he approaches the counsel table after a break. He points to her hair, asking if it's a new do, then smiles again when she nods her head. Little noises pass between them as he is seated.

After much cogitation, Wingate finally delivers his ruling on the admissibility of Gilbert's statement. Briefly, without much explanation, he declares that it will not be admitted. Seale smiles and pats Nester on the back.

The long-awaited moment of Edwards's return to the stand is not yet at hand. Instead, the prosecution intends to present witnesses to describe what a violent racist Seale was back in the sixties. Fitzgerald had tried to get this sort of "Klan" or "reign of terror" evidence into the Avants trial, but the judge wouldn't allow it. Here, to better the chances of its admission, the government is alleging a Klan conspiracy to kidnap and murder Dee and Moore. Such a charge was designed to allow the government to prove that Seale was a member of the Klan, that the Klan conspired to wage a reign of terror against blacks, and that Seale participated in both the conspiracy and the terror. It's a backdoor way of getting in otherwise prohibited "character" evidence.

So, coming on stage now, in a series of sometimes frightening and other times sad testimonies, will be a parade of true Mississippi characters, reminiscent of some of the odd ducks in the jury pool.

R. W. Middleton, seventy-seven, is a burly, outspoken man who seems completely at ease on the stand. When the listening device hooked around his ear isn't working properly, he casually signals the clerk to bring him a new one. In 1963 Middleton was a part-time preacher in Natchez when Archie Prather offered him the use of a house on his land in Bunkley if he would become the Bunkley Baptist Church's regular preacher. Middleton moved into the ramshackle house on a bluff in the Homochitto National Forest, and within a few months he had fixed it up and become good friends with James Ford Seale. Both men were young and loved guns. They would strap on a pair of pistols and compete in fast-draw contests in the woods behind Middleton's house. Middleton was moved by his new friend's generosity; one time, after borrowing Middleton's car, Seale returned it with four brand-new tires on it.

Middleton calmly tells the jury of his brief history with James Ford Seale. On the front porch of his house, he had mounted a vice to sharpen his axe. James Seale came by one day and asked if he could use the vice to saw off a double barrel shotgun. Middleton wondered aloud why he would want to mess up a good gun. "House protection," Seale responded. He added that a man could do a lot of harm with a sawed-off shotgun if he "walked into a nigger juke joint and started spraying shot." When Middleton mentioned he could go to jail for that, Seale shrugged; they'd have to catch him first.

Middleton, who had four kids, didn't much like the idea of integration himself—he feared his children would be wrongly influenced—but he was a man of God, and hatred based on race was against his beliefs. As it turned out, Middleton's tenure as preacher at the Bunkley Baptist Church was a short one. Archie Prather taught adult Sunday school, and one Sunday, as Middleton watched in dismay and James Seale grinned in approval, Prather interrupted the lesson and began talking about how bad the niggers had gotten since they had learned they would be going to school with white children. He'd heard how several ladies in the church were getting scared to go out because blacks were following them down the road. Prather told the ladies, "If you ever get worried, you tell me, and I'll get in the trunk of your car with the lid open and shoot every one of those niggers."

On the following Sunday, Middleton told the congregation from the pulpit that he didn't approve of this kind of talk in church. He didn't like integration either, but church was no place to talk of killing. If you must talk about it, do it in your home.

Prather protégé James Seale turned on Middleton like a rabid dog. Seale told the preacher to get off Prather's property and out of town because the community didn't want him around. Middleton moved to Roxie. Seale showed up at his new house with a couple of his brothers, determined to whip his ass, but was scared off by another preacher. Middleton got restraining orders against the Seales. Finally, he moved far away—James Seale was just too dangerous.

Fitzgerald projects on the screen a color photo of two men dressed in Klan robes: one in white with a red cross on his chest, the other in red with a white cross on his chest. Both are wearing pointed hoods. Middleton identifies the man in the red robe as Jack Seale, James's older brother, considered by some to be even more violent than James.

Middleton brings a moment of humor to his role in the play. When defense attorney George Lucas is cross-examining him about the wisdom of helping Seale saw off his shotgun, Middleton objects. "Sir, you're leading the witness."

Lucas hesitates.

"Sir, I know a leading question when I hear one," Middleton repeats.

The audience laughs. Seale laughs. Even the judge, jurors, and lawyers laugh. For a moment, it seems as if everyone in the courtroom is all one family, sorting out a difficult problem with one of its members, but with goodwill and the best of intentions.

"How about I ask the questions and you answer them," Lucas suggests politely, trying to reestablish a little decorum.

"Okay, but keep the questions straight."

CHAPTER 29

To hang the Klan robe on the shoulders of James Ford Seale once and for all, the prosecution brings to the stand a small, round-faced woman. In her late forties, wearing glasses, short black hair in bangs, Linda Luallen is one of the younger witnesses in the trial. She seems on the verge of falling apart the moment she sits down. A few sentences into her story, she begins to weep. Through the tears, she says that she had been married to Seale's son, James Ford Seale Jr., for twenty-five years. She had been close to her mother-in-law, Shirley, and always got along well with her father-in-law, whom she called "Pop."

Pop had no use for blacks, whom he always called niggers. He proudly told her stories of his days in the Klan. At family gatherings, he showed an 8 mm film he had shot of Klan rallies in Natchez and Jackson. She had seen the film at least twenty times.

In 1976, before they were married, Junior took Linda by his parents' house one day when they were gone. He walked to a closet and took out his dad's "Klan suit" and showed it to her. She dabs her eyes with a Kleenex, and Fitzgerald asks her if she would like a moment. She declines. When her father-in-law moved into a trailer, he gave his guns, including a sawed-off shotgun, to Junior.

On cross, Nester sets out to destroy the witness's credibility. Linda insists she has no axe to grind with the family, although after Junior had thrown her out of the house, she had threatened harm to him and his girlfriend. She had taken a box cutter to the waterbed, *their* waterbed, and also used it to cut her own image out of the family photos. Junior had been abusive to her during the marriage—he had threatened to shoot her, for one thing—and she had had to seek psychiatric help for depression. Yes, she had done drugs for about three years in high school, but it was Junior who had gotten her into them.

Crying softly, she admits that Junior and his new woman had obtained a restraining order against her. When she left the house, she moved right in with another man. "I did what I had to do."

The audience wants it over with. Whatever benefit was gained by the image of a robe in Seale's closet or a film of marching Klansmen has been overwhelmed by the sight and sound of this poor woman spilling her guts to the world. Nester relents, and the woman is excused.

The jury doesn't hear that Luallen believes that all three of Pop's children think that he killed their mother. Or that Pop disowned his grandchild, one of her sons, after he married a black woman.

Mississippi is hook and bullet country. Fishing and hunting are more than pastimes; they're tribal rituals, particularly in Southwest Mississippi, the most rural part of the state, where you can hunt birds and animals in the heavily forested countryside nearly year round: doves in the fall, turkeys in the spring, and squirrels, deer, rabbits, coons, wild hogs, and occasionally black bear in between. Hunting camps—wood shacks with stoves, bunks, and a fridge—are set up in the forest, and hunters camp in them for days, even weeks, fishing or tracking and shooting prey during the day and cleaning the game and drinking and telling stories at night. Men hunt the same forests that their daddies, granddaddies, and even great-granddaddies once hunted. Clyde Seale had set aside a few acres for a hunting camp on his land next to an old dairy farm outside Meadville.

Donald Irby worked in a car dealership in Natchez with James Junior in the early nineties. He testifies that on four or five occasions he joined Junior at the old camp to go deer hunting. Junior would brag that his daddy was in the Klan and liked to kill niggers. Senior, when he showed up at the camp, talked about how much he hated niggers, wouldn't piss on them, and claimed that he would be happy killing them for a living. In fact, he used to drive down the roads of Franklin County shooting niggers indiscriminately. Once, while crop dusting, he swooped down on a nigger riding a tractor, and crashed the plane in the field. Senior acted like he could get away with it all because he was a deputy sheriff.

Irby claimed that James Senior had told a story at the hunting camp about picking up two black kids in Franklin County and taking them to a local wooded area to give them a whipping. He also threw some black folks in the Mississippi River. Irby recalled that Junior and his mother always seemed scared around his daddy. Junior told him later he was convinced his daddy had murdered his mother.

But the jury doesn't hear all of this. What it hears from Irby on the stand is that Seale Senior bragged at the hunting camp that he was a constable with a license to kill in Franklin County and that he liked to talk about driving the country roads shooting blacks. Defense counsel George Lucas, on cross, tries to brush the comments off as nothing more than "BS," but the image is taking shape of a man who would shoot and kill blacks not only out of an almost genetic hatred for them but also out of a need to have something to brag about to his tribe.

CHAPTER 30

The Supreme Court ordered the integration of public schools in the South in 1954. Mississippi made little effort to comply by dismantling its "separate but equal" school system, and by 1964 the state still had shown little intention of doing so. Politicians ran successfully on a platform that Mississippi schools would never be integrated. When Gov. Ross Barnett cried, "I love Mississippi!" to a stadium full of football fans the day before James Meredith was to enroll at Ole Miss, everyone, supporters or not, understood what he meant. Ernest Parker proudly wore a "Never" button on his lapel in 1966 when he testified in front of the House Un-American Activities Committee, which was investigating the Klan and the murders of Moore and Dee. "Never" could have been the state slogan.

In 1963, President Kennedy proposed legislation intended to virtually wipe out Jim Crow in the South. Not only did the law outlaw segregated schools, but it gave the attorney general the authority to sue states that failed to integrate their schools; equally cataclysmically, the law outlawed discrimination in all public accommodations, meaning theaters, restaurants, bus stations, swimming pools—any place open to the public. Both of Mississippi's senators, James O. Eastland and John C. Stennis, joined in a southern filibuster against the bill. Some historians speculate that President Kennedy's assassination provided the impetus for the law's eventual passage under the stewardship of President Johnson. The passage of this law by a Democratic Congress and Democratic president spelled doom not only for Jim Crow but for the Democratic Party in the South as well.

As a young man, Seale might well have been tracking the legislation's tortured progress through the House and Senate in the spring of 1964; he may well have felt that when the Senate broke the filibuster, it also broke the heart of the Old South. He may even have been thinking of the law and what it would mean in his life when he pulled his white Volkswagen to a stop alongside Henry Dee and Charles Moore outside of Meadville on the morning of May 2. It wasn't too late; it would never be too late. Scouring the county for Muslim guns was the Klan's job, but ordinary people needed to wake up to what was happening to their country.

Seale expressed his feelings in a letter to the *Franklin County Advocate* published on July 23, 1964, ten days after the initial discovery of the bodies. In the letter, Seale gives his view on school integration and the Civil Rights Act of 1964. He writes,

> The reason we have these Judases and communist garbage in our public offices is because we have too many so called American Citizens that sit on their big fat lazy bottoms watching a western on T.V., sucking a beer bottle and getting fat like a big hog, and when the news comes

on they change channels to get another western or gangster. Most of these so-called American people don't even register and vote, when asked to vote.

Seale wants the citizens to do what they always do when their government goes bad: vote the rascals out.

With the help of God, we the people, can win this battle by praying, fighting and resisting this bill to the fullest extent of Human ability and at election time by sticking together and voting an unpledged ticket and kicking all the rotten communist garbage out of our public office.

In the next sentence, he gets around to the phrase "the nigger." Positioning "the" before the word "nigger" to form the plural, rather than saying "niggers" or even "the niggers," adds a historically insulting tone to the word, as if (the) blacks were perhaps inanimate objects. It's why some people today object to the use of the phrase "the blacks" in a sentence, such as "The blacks now control Jackson city government."

The so-called Civil Rights Bill is supposed to help the nigger both North and South. It is supposed to help the nigger get equal schools, when in most places in the south they have better schools. It is supposed to give the nigger equal voting rights, when in the South, if a nigger is qualified to vote, he can, if not he is not turned away, the same applies to white.

Finally, he drives home the most fundamental fear: the taking of white women.

But the above things are not what they want, they want to eat in the white café, sleep in the white home, swim in the white pool, go to the white church, go to the white school. In short, they want to marry your white daughter, or live with her, the only thing they know.

Seale lays down the trump card: integration is contrary to the word of God. He quotes,

NEHEMIAH 13:23–26.
And I contended with them, and cursed them, and smote certain of them, and plucked off their hair and make them swear by God, saying, Ye shall not GIVE YOUR DAUGHTERS UNTO THEIR SONS, NOT TAKE THEIR DAUGHTERS UNTO YOUR SONS, OR FOR YOURSELVES.

In closing, he comes back not to the threat of "100 percent integration" but to the likelihood of a Communist takeover of the government.

The time is here and passing fast for the people of this great nation to fight and die for what is right, if you choose to live and die under communism dictatorship, may God have mercy on your souls.

Did Seale really believe in the Communist threat? Or was it just a technique to keep hammering into submission a lesser tribe than his own. In Mississippi, in the South, the threat was commonly used by political leaders as a way to coalesce the white vote: it's not so much the blacks that are the problem—we get along fine with 'em—it's the

Communists behind the blacks. The attitude may seem extreme now, but it should be remembered that only a few years earlier, students in schools all over the country were crawling under their school desks in drills to avoid the blast of a Communist-launched nuclear bomb.

Perhaps Seale's letter to the residents of Franklin County was less a call to action than a confession, or at least an explanation for what he had done in the forest and along the banks of the Mississippi two and a half months earlier. Maybe in the secret chambers of his heart, Seale genuinely believed that he was entitled to recognition for what he had done, and this letter was a way of drawing attention to his deeds.

The prosecution seeks to introduce the letter; Nester, of course, fights its admission. Although the county clerk had authenticated the copy of the article in the *Franklin County Advocate* as true and accurate, who was to say that James Seale himself had actually written it? It proved nothing that his name happened to be at the bottom of the letter, along with his address: Rte. 2, Meadville, Mississippi.

The prosecution brought in the owner and editor of the newspaper, Mary Lou Webb, to authenticate the letter. Webb, well into her eighties, with an umbrella of stark white hair and bright, sharp eyes, had run the paper with her now deceased husband, David, since the '50s. In 1964 David was publicity director for the Americans for the Preservation of the White Race. The *Advocate* did not write of the missing black youths for two months after their disappearance in 1964. When their bodies were found, the paper declared in a small headline, "2 Local Negroes Thought Found in Miss. River."

In July 2005, after U.S. Attorney Dunn Lampton had reopened the Dee-Moore case, Webb wrote an editorial saying the paper was not going to cover the case. "The *Franklin County Advocate* has weighed the issues and decided not to 'revisit' the 1960s racial incidents which took place in this county and southwest Mississippi," Webb wrote. "The editor sees no new evidence—no reason—to put a new generation through painful memories. . . . Halfway around the world our young people are dying because their young people were not allowed to forgive and forget. Let that not be the legacy we leave our children."

On the stand, Webb is adamant that Seale was the author of the letter in question. In those days, the paper wouldn't publish a letter unless the writer hand-delivered it and paid $25. She personally knew Seale to be in the Klan because he had told her he was. He had bragged about it and even threatened her. Once he came into the newspaper office to challenge her and her husband over some of the articles the paper had carried. "I'm a member of the Klan," he said. "We don't like some of the things you're publishing. It's not very healthy for you." She pointed to Seale's anger as proof that her publication was fair and balanced—you don't piss off the Klan for nothing.

If this story is true, Webb was among the few whites in Franklin County willing or inclined to run afoul of the Klan. Although membership in the White Knights in Franklin County in the mid-sixties was estimated at only 60 to 70 men—5,000 in the entire state—the prevailing view is that most of the residents were, to one degree or another, sympathetic to the Klan. It is an uncertain truth. If you were a farmer, sawmill worker, or housewife in rural

Mississippi in 1964, and you made your negative views of
the Klan or its activities known, you could bring harm to
your family as well as yourself. Being in favor of segregation was not always the same as being in favor of violence
to maintain it.

Highway Patrol detectives Rex Armistead and Donald
Butler were not in the Klan. Neither were they scared of
the Klan. When they uncovered a patrolman in the Klan,
the detectives busted him. Both born in Mississippi, the
men were assigned to investigate the Klan in Southwest
Mississippi in 1964, a treacherous task given the strangle-
hold the Bunkley Klan had on Franklin County. On oc-
casion, the detectives couldn't get service in a local café or
gas pumped into their car at a Meadville station. People
yelled "nigger lover" at them as they drove the streets of
Natchez.

The two detectives were quickly introduced to the
"Seale boys," as they were called. There were a lot of them,
they were in the Klan, and they were violent. (Violence was
a Seale family tradition, one state cop would say.) Daddy
Clyde might have been the meanest of them all, but James
was a rogue and a bully. Not the smartest of the bunch, he
was the one out front with the threats and the guns. If pro-
voked, he might shoot the person or burn his house down.

One day Armistead got a message from a dispatcher to
call a certain pay phone, and when he did, the voice on the
other end said to him coolly, "Your little ol' blonde-haired
girl ain't going to make it home from school tomorrow."
Armistead, who had a twelve-year-old daughter, recognized the voice as that of James Seale. Living across the

river in Vidalia, Louisiana, Seale was driving a wood chip truck at the time, and you could come across him anywhere. Armistead got a police photo of Seale, stuck it on his visor, and waited.

In the spring of 1965, the Klan took out ads in the Natchez paper and stuck posters and telephone poles around town announcing the appearance of Klan Grand Wizard Robert Shelton at an upcoming public rally in Liberty Park. On the appointed day, the streets filled with hundreds of Klansmen in their robes. As the detectives turned a downtown corner in an unmarked police car, they spotted Seale and another man in their robes standing in front of the Eola Hotel holding cameras. The police car jerked to a stop. Seale walked over, pushed the camera in the detectives' faces, and began snapping pictures. The detectives jumped from the car and grabbed him. Armistead jerked the camera from Seale's hands and ripped the film from it. Seale yelled in their faces and threw a couple of punches. He knew his rights; he wasn't violating any law; the sidewalk was a public place.

Armistead claims today that he used only the "force necessary to effect an arrest" on Seale. Butler, who had had a cross burned on his lawn and admits to having had "a little violent session or two with the Klan," says that Seale's feet might have left the ground once or twice on the trip and that he might have got his butt kicked a few times in the sheriff's office while they were twisting him around to get the Klan robe off him. In any event, Seale was locked up and missed the march.

Later that day, the two detectives drove to a field near the Holiday Inn where a cross had been planted for an evening rally. Surrounded by Klansmen, the state car crept over the grass until it bumped into the cross, then slowly inched forward until the cross toppled to the ground with a thunk. "It was hot," Armistead says, thinking back on Klansmen's habit of hiding weapons under their robes, "but not a hand touched the state car."

Gov. Paul B. Johnson Jr. called Armistead into his office a few days later. The governor, who had stood in the doorway at Ole Miss with Ross Barnett to block Meredith and has been widely quoted as saying early in his career that the NAACP stands for "niggers, alligators, apes, coons and possums," nevertheless told Armistead that he and Butler were doing a good job of hassling the Klan. "Get your ass back down there and quit worrying. I've got the key to Parchman" (the infamous state penitentiary not far from Sumner).

In the trial, Armistead is scratched from the witness list because of inflammatory statements about the incident he had given to the *Clarion-Ledger* a few weeks earlier. Former detective Butler, now the deputy chief of the Mississippi Bureau of Narcotics, takes the stand to tell the jury of Seale's role in the bad old days of the Klan. He describes in a calm historian's voice life in Southwest Mississippi in 1964: the regular Klan burnings, beatings, and murders, the membership of law enforcement (sheriffs, constables, and Highway Patrol) in the Klan, the patrol's use of informants to infiltrate the organization, and of course his encounters with the Seale boys and the infamous Bunkley Klan. He tells the story of the incident in Natchez when a Klan-robed James Seale took his picture and of the time he witnessed Seale packing a pistol at a peaceful voter-registration march in Lafayette.

Another ancient warrior, former FBI agent James Ingram, takes the stand to verify phone records showing that on the afternoon of the murders, phone calls were made from Clyde Seale's house to the homes of Jack Seale and Ernest Parker, as testified to by Edwards. Ingram, who has been keeping track of the government witnesses like a mother hen, strides purposefully to the stand. Unlike some of the other old agents, he speaks clearly, confidently, and without hesitation, and you can imagine the determined young agent who went after Seale in 1964. Hammering a nail in Seale's coffin would cap off a remarkable career in law enforcement. Unfortunately, after Ingram's and several other witnesses' testimony, the judge finds that the records contained too many levels of hearsay.

James Ford Seale might be wasting away at the defense table, but several days of testimony by the parade of figures from his dark past have transformed him. James Ford Seale now wears a pistol on his hip and is draped in a bright red robe with a white cross on the chest. He rides without fear in the dark of night, burning churches, threatening whites, and shooting blacks. The present is now 1964. *Mississippi Burning*, with voices humming mournfully in the background, flames crackling and leaping against a black sky, might as well be playing on a giant screen behind the judge.

CHAPTER 31

The prosecution calls Thomas Moore to the stand. The only other child of Mazie Moore, who raised her boys on welfare of $12 a week and what she earned cooking and cleaning in a white woman's house, he is the son who followed her advice and tried to forget what happened to his brother. He moved on and made something of his life, spending thirty years in the U.S. Army, where he saw the world.

Thomas is the true tragic figure of this play, and he is called now not because he knows anything of the crime or James Ford Seale but because he can enable the jury to feel the lives of Charles and Henry that could have been, then talk of the pain and suffering of those left behind. There is no use objecting to his taking the stand. Courts routinely allow such testimony as part of the prosecution's story; the defense can only point out that it doesn't connect the defendant to the crime. Seale sits a few feet from Thomas Moore, wearing his usual expressionless look, his face absent, as one prospective juror had put it, any hint of remorse.

Moore, in a black T-shirt and slacks, rises from his usual place in the front row and passes through the gate and across the room to the witness stand. He looks out on the courtroom, and his bald head, trimmed goatee, and darkly encircled, intense eyes give him a slightly menacing aura. He speaks in short bursts, with brief silences in between, in a rhythm that is sometimes hard to follow. He talks proudly of his career as a soldier in the U.S. Army and of his experience fighting as a reconnaissance squad leader, sniper, and gunner on a Huey gunship in three major battles in Vietnam.

You see that this is how Moore made it through life after his brother's murder, by living the regulated, hardshell existence of a professional soldier, by willingly facing death himself.

Thomas relaxes and rolls a little in his chair as he describes his younger brother. Charles, Nub, his mother's favorite, was a good boy, better than he, and more ambitious. Thomas even had to fight his fights for him in the schoolyard. Thomas stayed behind a year to try for a college football scholarship, and the two brothers ran against each other for class president their senior year. Charles won. Thomas tells how both he and his brother got their four top front teeth knocked out playing football. Thomas first, then Charles a year later, both by cleats. Their mamma got dental plates made for them.

You watch for a rapid blinking, a sucked-in breath, any sign of distress, but there is nothing, only the staccato bursts and the silences. One thing Moore makes perfectly clear: neither Charles nor Henry had anything to do with civil rights. That stuff wasn't going on in Franklin County, no guns, none of that, as far as he knew. They were up to nothing that could have brought this down upon them. No sir.

Moore hunches forward a little and looks directly at Fitzgerald as he recounts how he was playing ping-pong in the barracks at Fort Hood when the news came on that two bodies had been discovered in the Mississippi River. He didn't pay much attention; he figured it was the civil rights workers in Philadelphia.

"It just wilted mamma," Moore continues, straightening a little. It broke her heart that there was no body for the casket, that she couldn't see her boy one last time. As for himself—he's had hard times, bad times. He fought booze. He had nightmares in the army, and he still does, to this day. His brother would visit him in Vietnam in his dreams and ask why? He doesn't know why.

The need to listen very closely to what Thomas is saying renders the courtroom tense and still. His death motivated me, the retired soldier intones. I pushed hard and rose to a G-9. I got two bachelor's degrees, and I had his name put on one of the diplomas. He pushed me to be all that I could be, all that I wanted to be. I miss him now. I will always miss him.

So, Thomas has lived for both himself and Charles—no wonder he is so strong and looks so exhausted. Whatever happens here in this courtroom or afterwards, for the rest of his life, that look of stillness in his eyes will always be there. Watching him solemnly from the first row is Thomas's late-in-life son, Jeffrey, who so resembles a young Charles.

"All rise!" The command jolts the mesmerized courtroom. The exodus from the room is solemn as the present slowly seeps back into consciousness. It's Friday afternoon, and court is over for the day, for the week. The second act seems finished, but the story's wandered so far from the main theme of guilt or innocence that there's no feel for what's coming next. Surely, it must be time on Monday for Edwards's reappearance. It seems so long ago that he sat in that chair and asked for forgiveness.

CHAPTER 32

Not all Mississippi is tied into the redemption drama being played out in the capital city. To the west, in the vast and timeless Delta, the rhythms of the past throb on almost in spite of the present. Highway 61, the Blues Highway, cuts through the town of Cleveland, the home of old bluesman Cadillac John, who has lived his life in the Delta, working in cotton fields, playing the harp and singing about women and hard times.

Cadillac hasn't heard about the case of James Ford Seale, although he's picked up a little about a few of the old Klansmen going to jail in recent years. He recalls Emmett Till, but he has little interest in knowing about what's going on with the case now. Cadillac has lived his life free of most of that, and at eighty-three he has few regrets. All you can do is sweat and try to get what you can, and when you got nothing or nobody, that's what you sing about. When he thinks about slavery and Jim Crow days and the plight of blacks in the Delta, his head tilts to the side. "My thing has always been getting by, and about women."

He got his name from an old Cadillac he owned. He had parked it outside a supermarket one day, and when he went to start it up, it backfired, sounding like the blast of a shotgun. From that day on, it was Cadillac John. The car is long since gone. Like his only wife. Whooooboy. He came home one day, and she was gone, and she had took everything with her: the furniture, the radio, the pots and pans, even the drapes. The drapes were the hardest. Leave a man exposed to the bright sun. He lay down on the bathroom floor to sleep. The next day, he scraped up a few dollars and walked down to the drugstore and bought a harp. He went home, crawled in his closet, and started playing on it until he found a sound, a feeling—he didn't know what it was or where it came from—and the weight started lifting a little from him, although the tears kept rising.

Cadillac John grew up on the plantation where his parents sharecropped. He was one of ten kids, and the family moved from plantation to plantation, wherever they could work the best deal. From sun up to sun down, he and the other kids chopped cotton and worked the plough behind the mules right along with the adults.

He never learned to read music, but he picked up gospel, and he and his three brothers formed a little group—the Four Nolden Brothers—and sang on street corners for spare change. They got good enough to sing on station WGRN in Greenwood at 9:30 on Sunday mornings.

But there was little money in singing gospel—only a few coins others might drop in your hat—so he started blowing harp and singing the blues and writing his own songs. He played at the juke joints scattered around Sunflower County, sometimes by himself, often with others. He sang about hard times, and he sang about love, and he sang about women. The day his wife left—somewhere in the fifties or sixties, he wasn't sure—he was working at a gas station, and a man told him someone was up at his house, but he couldn't mess with his job. When he got home, she was gone. "Brenda Faye, baby, please come back home to me," he sang in his closet. He was trying to keep his mind off her, but no sooner had he quit blowing than his mind went right back to her.

One night at a joint he was singing so hard about Brenda Faye it brought another man down. John didn't know his singing was bothering anyone, until two men at a table near the front fell apart and started crying. One man was drunk, and he kept calling out, "My wife is gone, and I don't know where she's at." The second guy told those around him to make John stop singing, but they took the man away instead, still crying. If Cadillac had known how bad the man was hurting, he wouldn't have sung so much about his own pain.

In those days, Cadillac John sometimes played on small stages with another young blues player, Riley King. Riley was a good singer, but there wasn't much to him. He played guitar and sang at a juke joint run by a woman named Bit, and one night he hollered out a song called "Don't Cry Baby You Know You Been So Mean to Me." The song was so good that Cadillac John almost cried himself. After Riley moved on to the city and changed his name to B. B. King, Cadillac never heard from him again.

Charley Booker would come to the house and listen to a blues show on the radio. Charley could play that guitar all by himself, particularly when he had a drink in him. He used to let John into the little joint he owned in Leland for nothing, and people were jammed up in there drinking and dancing through the night. In those days, guns sometimes went along with the corn whiskey, and things could go bad. One night a woman came after Charley with a knife. He fought back with his guitar, and she sliced the strings off it. Charley could play all night long without a break.

"I would see Charley Booker playing down on the street corner, tears rollin' down his cheeks. Charley had to carry a handkerchief to keep the tears away—it just got to him. The further you go, the better the feeling gets, and he had got into it."

That was the old-time blues, the original Delta blues, and it's the way Cadillac John still sings them. Straight out. With a soft, sometimes beseeching voice, to a steady, thumping rhythm, he plays the harp and sings about mules, and automobiles, and women, and hard times. One song, on his only CD, entitled "Crazy About You (But You Don't Care Nothing About Me)," is about inviting a woman to climb up and ride his mule. Then there's "My Baby Left Me This Morning (She Didn't Even Tell Me Goodbye)," which doesn't mention Brenda Faye but sure sounds like it's about her. He sings "Bottle Up and Go," although he's never been a drinker.

John never made it big, maybe because he likes to stay close to home. A large map of the Delta blues country hangs on his wall. The map names him—there's a star next to Sunflower, where he was born—along with Robert Johnson, Honey Boy Edwards, Big John Murphy, Doc Terry, Junior Kimble, and the rest. He is interviewed occasionally in blues magazines, and you can feel the blues even in his spoken words:

I'll tell you another thing. A man, if he got him a family and is all right, he don't need no close male friends. Listen to me good. You do not need them. 'Cause they ain't there for your good. They'll hurt you. Eat you up. Cut your throat. You know, with your lady, you don't need nobody around there. It's best just to keep it like it is. I'm just telling the truth. That's right. 'Cause when you gone, he's the boss. I'm telling you now. I've been through this stuff. I get a chance, I want to put a song out about that. (*Blues Revue*, August/September 2007)

That song, it seems, will tell the rest of the story of Cadillac John Nolden and Brenda Faye.

Now, John lives in a small apartment with Crystal, a gospel singer. He seems content, but the blues still burn in his weary eyes. It's not about the Klan, oppression, or redemption. His voice drops as he thinks back over the years and sums them up. "Oooh," he says. "Don't fall in love too deep too quick, 'cause a woman'll break your heart sometimes."

ACT III

CHAPTER 33

The third and final act of this play within a play begins in the third week of the trial. There have been only seven days of actual performance, the rest spent selecting, arguing, deciding, or waiting, and although the drama has been thick and sometimes intense, the substance of guilt and innocence has been rather thin. Two young black men were kidnapped and murdered forty-three years ago; Charles Edwards says James Ford Seale told him he did it; Seale was a member of the Klan and a violent man; therefore, Seale must be the kidnapper and killer.

The prosecution has only a few more witnesses on its list, and although the defense has endorsed seven witnesses, the guess is that it will call only a few. It's hard to dispute facts forty-three years old; it is hard to disprove hearsay without the alleged sayer getting on the stand to deny it. So the defense will probably contest a few facts and fall back on the myriad weaknesses in the government's case, the main one being the lying soul of the only witness connecting Seale to the crime.

Thomas Moore concluded the second act searingly and his exit Friday afternoon seemed to be his finale. Thus, it's something of a surprise when he appears first on the stand Monday morning. A bit of a glitch has developed for the prosecution over the weekend. The CBC documentary chronicling Thomas Moore and producer David Ridgen's 2005 journey through Southwest Mississippi in search of Moore and Dee's murderers debuted on MSNBC on Saturday night. (The *Jackson Free Press* also published an excellent series of articles on the journey.) On Friday the judge had informed the jury of the showing and warned them not to view it. (This infuriated Jeannie Seale, who thought it revealed the judge's bias against her husband because it was actually a covert invitation to watch.) The film shows Thomas Moore approaching Edwards at his church on a Sunday morning and thrusting a manila envelope at him. Inside the envelope, the voice-over informs us, is the complete FBI report, including Edward Gilbert's 1964 statement. Here, then, could be the long-missing proof that Edwards's story had come not from what Seale had told him but from what Gilbert had told the FBI.

On the stand to talk about the incident, Moore tells the jury of his journey of redemption: He had come to Mississippi in July 2005 to confront his own past. He spent twenty-three months actively "on the ground" searching for his brother and Henry Dee's killers. One Sunday morning he had gone to the Bunkley Baptist Church to confront Edwards and get the truth from him. He strode across the lawn to Edwards, standing by the door of the country church, and said he had something for him to read.

"Who are you?" Edwards asked.

"I'm the brother of Charles Moore," he said.

"I did not kill your brother," Edwards said. "I had nothing to do with that."

"I didn't say you did," Moore responded. He handed him the manila envelope with the documents and asked if he had helped pick the boys up. Instead of answering, Edwards told him to get off the church property. Moore left, with the camera running.

Nester wants to show the jury the portion of the film where Edwards denies his involvement in the murders as a further example of his habitual lying. The judge allows it. After Moore leaves the stand, the jury watches the clip of Moore's encounter with Edwards.

Finally, the action flows back to the center ring. Edwards, dressed formally in a green blazer and slacks, strides through the door. He pulls the witness chair out, sits in it, and waits expectantly for the show to begin. U.S. Attorney Dunn Lampton immediately spots the change in Edwards's demeanor. When last here, he was nervous and uncertain. Today, his color is high, his voice firm, and he holds himself with a relaxed confidence. Lampton figures the apology to the families, and their acceptance of it, has brought about this transformation. Edwards's glance across the courtroom at the defendant, who has been watching him intently with his chin tucked in like a bird's, is unwavering, perhaps even a little sympathetic. After all these years of living a lie, he is right with God, as right as he can get, and now, as a redeemed Christian, perhaps he can worry about the soul of James Ford Seale.

Nester has thoroughly promulgated the notion that everything Edwards claims Seale told him he could have learned from other sources. Fitzgerald needs to rebut this argument. On redirect, she gets Edwards to deny that he read the report handed to him by Thomas Moore at the door of the church. She has argued that Gilbert's statement did not contain three critical facts included in Edwards's testimony: the route from the farm to the river, the search of the church, and the order in which the boys were dropped in the water. She now needs to insure that the jury can find that the two youths were taken across the state line and that they were alive when they crossed it, and she needs to make sure that the jury can find these facts from Edwards's direct knowledge—direct in that he either observed the events himself or heard about it from Seale's mouth.

She walks her star witness through the facts and asks the source of each. He answers question by question that either he was there and witnessed it or Seale told him about it.

Fitzgerald asks Edwards to tell the jury about a recent incident in his church.

"I told them [his congregation] that I was a deacon in the church and that I'd step down if they wanted me to, or I'd quit teaching Sunday school—I had a Sunday school class—if they wanted me to, or either—I'd do anything, but I wouldn't quit coming to church or quit supporting my pastor. And they voted unanimously—"

Nester interrupts with a hearsay objection, but the rest of his answer is clear: his church has forgiven him, still loves him.

"Did you ask forgiveness from the family?" Fitzgerald asks—an irrelevant question.

"I did," Edwards says. "It was the best thing that has come out of the case for me."

Within the few minutes since he walked in and sat down, Edwards has transformed from the habitually lying originator of the crimes into a sinner who has confessed in a house of God and sought forgiveness from the flesh. In this deeply Christian land, Edwards has been raised to a status above that of the ordinary man. His beatification has gone off without a hitch, and there is nothing Nester can do about it. She passes on further questions.

This onstage conversion of a sinner into a redeemed man leads an observer to reflect on the nature of Mississippi's path to redemption. Technically, redemption is not possible; it presumes a return to an earlier, sinless state, which Mississippi never had. Mississippi's movement is strictly forward. But even so, how will Mississippi know when it has finally crossed over the river? Must there be some sort of cultural confession? A pleading for forgiveness? If the past indeed will never die in Mississippi, can it not at least loosen its grip on the present and give the future a chance?

One native, an educated man, asks the question a different way: What does the country want out of Mississippi? What's it going to take? He answers his own question.

"Nothing," he says. "It'll take nothing. It'll go on forever. You guys need Mississippi down on the bottom, just like the whites in Mississippi needed the blacks down on the bottom. Human nature, I guess."

Not that Mississippi doesn't hinder its cause, intentionally or otherwise, with its own actions. In 2001, a proposition was put before the citizens to adopt a newly designed flag that did not contain the Confederate Stars and Bars. The voters rejected the proposal by an overwhelming 64 percent, with 90 percent of white voters voting against it and 95 percent of black voters voting in favor of it. Some whites say the new design wasn't any good; others say the new flag was a slap against their heritage. Many blacks, not surprised at the outcome, just shake their head at white voters' stubbornness.

As Edwards works his way through the crowded hallway to the elevator, a black minister and several cousins of the victims take him aside to tell him they, too, forgave him for his misdeeds.

"Thank you," Edwards says sincerely, pausing for a moment. "I appreciate that."

On the steps outside the courthouse, Thomas Moore tells the TV cameras that he believes his brother is up there looking down on them. "I've done everything I can do," he intones forcefully, "regardless of what happens."

CHAPTER 34

The prosecution, with its last few witnesses, seeks to corroborate and shore up Edwards's testimony. It calls the FBI agent who polygraphed Edwards in 2006. Special Agent T. J. Spniewski has a difficult name to pronounce, but he is movie-star handsome and very smooth. He testifies that Edwards showed deception on only two questions: "Do you know for sure what happened to those boys that day?" and "Do you know for sure what James Seale did to those boys that day?" The agent says he told Edwards after the test that he hadn't been truthful and reminded him that the penalty for lying to an FBI agent was up to ten years in prison and a $250,000 fine. Spniewski kept at him for forty-five minutes, and gradually Edwards's denials grew weaker. Finally, he admitted he knew for sure what had happened and scribbled out a one-page statement of the facts as Seale had related them to him.

Two more people take the stand to speak for Seale. The first is FBI agent Edward Putz, one of the agents who arrested Seale in 1964. White-haired, tall, and lanky, he identifies and reads from a written statement recounting what Seale told the officers on his arrest. Another agent had said to Seale, "You didn't even give them a decent burial. We know you did it; the Lord above knows you did it." Seale replied, "Yes, but I'm not going to admit it. You're going to have to prove it."

Although Putz took this statement as an admission, it could be seen as the arrogant challenge of a Klansman who couldn't conceive of an officer of the law as constituting a serious threat to his freedom. "Yes" doesn't sound like the way Seale would talk in those circumstances. The remark sounds like, "Yeah, I ain't saying nothing. Go dig for it," in which case he's simply telling the despised feds to fuck off. If nothing else, however, the comment reinforces Seale's mouthy mad-boy image. It takes some sort of an attitude, a Klan sort of attitude, to lip off to two FBI agents like that.

At the end of his testimony, Putz, sturdy as an ancient lodgepole pine, looks up at the judges and asks, "Can I go home?"

Court never starts on time. It always begins at least fifteen minutes late, often half an hour or more. Wingate, after one delay that consumed most of the afternoon, ventured down from his throne to apologize and explain in some detail that he had gone to the eye doctor over lunch for an examination. It's his eyes' fault: his pupils didn't dilate properly, and he had to wait until they returned to normal because, as he had explained to the doctor, he had to be able to read all the motions and briefs in this trial.

A federal judge owes the spectators no explanation as to how or why he runs the courtroom the way he does, but Wingate's chosen this moment to show the audience that he's indeed mortal, just as they are. The audience responds appropriately, chuckling or nodding at the right moments, pleased to be taken into the judge's confidence.

The next secondhand collection of words out of Seale's mouth is even weaker evidence of his guilt than the last. Mark Stucky, another tall, lanky FBI agent, although not ancient like Putz and most of the others, was in on Seale's arrest in January 2007. He testifies that when Seale answered the knock on his motor home door, he identified himself as an FBI agent and said he wanted to talk to Seale about the events of 1964. Seale shut the door. When the agent repeated that he wanted to talk to him, Seale cracked the door and demanded, "Am I under arrest?" undoubtedly planning after the cop answered no to order him imperiously off his property.

Stucky said, "Yes, you are," and proceeded to read him his Miranda warnings. The agent used an old ploy to trick a confession out of a suspect: confront him with the facts of his guilt, with a few inaccuracies, and see if he wants to correct them. He said to Seale, we know you picked the boys up and took them to the forest; we know you beat them to death and took them in a car across the river; we know you put them in a boat and dumped them in the water. Seale at first insisted that he didn't know what the agent was talking about. Then, after the agent kept up with the "facts," Seale said there was no point in his saying anything because "you obviously know it all already." Although this statement might sound more like "screw you" than "yeah, I did it," it's still one more stick, however slender, tossed in the tinderbox beneath Seale's feet.

The prosecution rests. Nester seeks immediate dismissal of the charges for lack of a speedy trial and insufficient evidence, both of which motions the judge quickly and predictably denies.

It is now time for the defense, the first scene of the final act, but few anticipate that much drama will come from it. There is no alibi witness to place Seale in another state or city on May 2, 1964, no expert witness to say the fingerprints under the duct tape didn't belong to him, no forensic scientist to say the bones found on the river bottom weren't those of two young men. But the defense needs to put somebody on the stand or risk looking weak. The tension is building for the play to wind up.

The defense calls its first witness. Brother Don Seale takes the stand to bolster the theory that the cops beat James while he was in custody in 1964 and therefore his "confession" should be excluded. Wearing a checkered blue shirt and square glasses, Don Seale drops a blue seed dealer's cap onto the witness stand before taking the oath. Back then, he only lived three to four hundred yards from Seale, and when he saw his brother the day after his arrest, James had red spots on his face and injuries to his ribs—Don doesn't know from what. He had spoken to his brother only twice in the last twenty-five years due to a "family matter."

On cross, Fitzgerald seizes quickly on the "family matter," and Don Seale explains that when his mother died, James and brother Jack took all of the stuff that belonged to their daddy. He denies ever being a member of the Klan; he's not sure whether James was.

Fitzgerald then reads a quote from a recent FBI interview in which Don Seale supposedly told the agents how things were back in 1964: "You could go over there and call them niggers, and they'd laugh. They all know their place in life." The witness denies making the statement. Don Seale seems a net minus for the defense: James Seale, in addition to all else, now stole his daddy's stuff from his two brothers. It's a wonder Fitzgerald hasn't found a way to get in the rumors that he killed his first wife.

Jeannie Seale slips out of the courtroom as Don Seale finishes testifying. The way she heard it, Don hadn't known that brother Gene, a farmer outside Meadville, and James had bought the Bunkley property from their parents, so he had thought he would get a share when they died and was pissed when he didn't. She tries to talk to Don in the hallway, but he will have none of it: he tells her he doesn't care if he never sees or speaks to his brother again for the rest of his life. The words, the attitude, hurt Jeannie. To her, family is everything.

On top of all else, her James, who swore to her again and again that he did not kidnap those boys, is very ill. He's on pure oxygen in the jail, and during the trial they've taken him to the hospital three times. He had been on 125 mg morphine patches for cancer pain, but the jail for some reason reduced his dose to 25 mg, and he went into withdrawal.

If Seale were to die at this point, the charges would be dismissed. Even if he is convicted, the judgment will not be final until his appeal has been concluded, and that will take over a year. Were he to die in the meantime, with Edwards now permanently immune, Thomas Moore and Thelma Collins would be denied justice, and Mississippi would lose the satisfaction of having at last provided it.

Chapter 35

The defense has two shots in its meager arsenal. The target in both instances is federal jurisdiction. Dee and Moore must have been taken alive across state lines. If the Klansmen killed them in the forest, then hauled the bodies to Natchez and across the river into Louisiana and dumped them in the Mississippi at Parker's Landing, the case will fail. The defense has heard stories from a few Franklin County locals about what really happened on that Saturday morning: the Klan never intended to kill the black youths; the men were beating and questioning them to find the guns, when they went too far and one of them fell over. Thinking him dead, the men killed the other one, and (like Romeo and Juliet) when the first one woke up, they had to kill him as well. (It seems somewhat logical that, if you know you are eventually going to kill two men, you would do it before transporting them in the back of a car fifty miles to a river.) Even if Nester has some evidence to support this version, it is not an alternative theory she can easily toss out. "Ladies and gentlemen of the jury, my client admits that he killed both of these young men, but he murdered them in the Homochitto National Forest. There-

fore, you must acquit." Nester and others on the defense
team have jokingly imagined putting Seale on the stand to
tell such a tale but never seriously considered it.

So Nester goes at the location issue sideways. The
prosecution had earlier called Dr. Steven Hayne, the state
pathologist. Hayne testified with a reasonable degree of
medical certainty that the cause of death was freshwater
drowning and the manner was homicide. Drowning would
establish that Dee and Moore had been alive when taken
across the state line. But since no soft tissue or organs
were attached to the bones, the defense challenged how
the pathologist could be at all certain that Dee and Moore
had drowned. Well, Hayne countered, he had listened to
Edwards's testimony about what Seale had told him.

That's not science, Nester had argued then, and today
she calls her own pathologist, who testifies quite convinc-
ingly that based on the evidence alone, which really amounts
to two piles of bones, there is no way to tell the cause of
death. The absence of injury to the bones—a bullet hole in
the skull or a chunk out of a rib—does not by itself establish
drowning as the cause.

The prosecution's evidence also does not establish
where the youths drowned. They could have drowned in a
river or pond in the national forest, although it seems un-
likely the Klansmen would have drowned the youths in a
local river or pond, then hauled them up to Parker's Island
and dumped their bodies in the Mississippi.

On cross, the pathologist admits that the fact that the
feet were bound with twine indeed suggests a homicide.
He also describes in detail the gruesome process of drowning: You are eventually forced to take a breath, but instead

of air you get a mouthful of water, which dilutes the blood salts and damages the heart and brain. You can last up to four minutes.

The defense fares little better with its second shot: an attack on the notion that the killers might have committed their grisly deeds without actually leaving Mississippi. Parker's Island sits somewhat in the middle of the backwater, and it is difficult to pinpoint the actual Mississippi-Louisiana state line. One witness, an employee of the U.S. Army Corps of Engineers, attempts to illustrate with maps how it would be possible to get to the island without entering Louisiana. A Vicksburg boat builder testifies that he has hauled people up the river to the island from Vicksburg.

The problem with this scenario, as with the first, is that it almost admits to the execution of the crime itself. Seale and the others killed Moore and Dee but drove to Vicksburg instead of Natchez and powered up the river to the island in a boat that never crossed some imaginary line into Louisiana. Will the jury really care about such a distinction?

Undaunted, Nester takes her final poke at Edwards's credibility. One of his lawyers, Walter Beasley, had told her on the phone after the indictment that Edwards was going to recant his written statement; he would say that Seale had never told him a thing about what happened after the forest. Out of the presence of the jury, she calls Beasley to the stand and asks him about the recantation. The judge disallows the answer on the grounds that it would violate the attorney-client privilege.

Nester announces solemnly that the defense rests its case. Wingate leans forward and addresses Seale directly.

"Mr. Seale, you understand that you have a right to testify in your own defense?"

The still courtroom watches as Seale rises slowly from his chair and wobbles to the podium.

"Yes, sir," he says softly.

"Are you waiving that right?"

"Yes, sir."

Seale wobbles back to the counsel table and sits with a small sigh. The courtroom pauses, waits for something more—from Seale, the judge, another witness—until it sinks in that the presentation of the evidence is now complete. All that remains is for counsel for each side to present their respective stories to the jury. The jury will buy one or the other, or neither.

CHAPTER 36

The courtroom is packed for closing arguments. Sixties movement people, relatives, media, students, writers, film-makers, law professors, and casual observers squeeze together on the benches. Burl Jones, who was whipped by the Klan and sent off to Chicago in the sixties and now lives in Natchez, and L. C. Dorsey, who grew up poor on a Delta plantation in the days of Jim Crow and returned after getting a doctorate at Howard University to run a community health clinic in Mound Bayou, sit quietly in the crowd. The young marshals, in their slacks and blazers, seem particularly attentive.

Good closings can make for high drama, with the lawyers veering back and forth from appealing to the emotions to appealing to the mind, pandering, pleading, reasoning, insisting, sometimes even bullying: This is the truth of what happened. Forget the other stuff. This is the truth.

Wingate, in his role as Moses, instructs the jury on how to go about discerning the truth: set bias and sympathy aside; do not consider what you think is wiser or better; follow the evidence, the facts. In other words, think, don't feel. Analyze, don't emote. The woman who wondered so articulately during jury selection how one is actually supposed to do that—separate feelings and biases from facts—is not on the jury, and none in the box dare challenge the hallowed fiction of the legal drama that thinking is some pure and isolated process. Apply the law to the evidence rationally and you will reach the correct result. A computer could do it.

Wingate-as-Moses lays out an even more hallowed fiction: the requirement of proof beyond a reasonable doubt to convict. How will you know if you do or don't have a reasonable doubt? If you would act without hesitation, as you would in making a personal decision, then you don't have reasonable doubt. He means that if you could find Seale guilty or innocent as easily or quickly as you would decide whether or not to accept a job offer or a marriage proposal, then you have no reasonable doubt. If you hesitate, if you go back and forth between the old job and the new job, getting married or not, then you have reasonable doubt.

Jurors are directed to use their intuition in one specific area: the credibility of witnesses. Do they impress you as honest? Or do they seem like liars? Do they have reasons to lie? And beware a witness granted immunity (like Edwards), for he has an obvious reason to lie. Which isn't to say you can't believe him, if you choose to, if things match up, but be careful of him.

Finally, Judge Wingate reminds the jury not to look to him or anything he's said or done during the trial as they decide the defendant's guilt or innocence. He has no opinion on the facts.

Each side has two hours. The prosecution goes first and last; the defense gets squeezed in the middle. U.S. Attorney

Dunn Lampton, the youthful-looking local boy, dressed in black suit and white shirt, leads off for the prosecution, and in true country lawyer fashion, he goes right for the emotional gut.

He asks the jurors to slip inside the skins of the two victims: Imagine you are at the farm and James Seale tapes your mouths shut and puts you in the trunk of the red Ford. It would be dark in there, you would have all this time to think, and you would be terrified and wonder, Why? Why? When the car stopped, you might, for a moment, feel relief, thinking it was over, that you'd be released and allowed to go home, for you hadn't done anything wrong. But it only gets worse. You see the river, you see Seale and Parker tie the engine block to your friend, Henry, and then you hear chains rattle, a motorboat sputtering, and the splash of the water as Henry drops in. You hear the sounds of the boat as it comes back for you, and when you look in the eyes of your captors, seeking pity or release, you pray, and maybe you wish you would be shot, a better death than being thrown in the dark, muddy backwaters of the Mississippi. As you go over, you hold your breath and struggle against the chains. When you finally take a breath, your lungs fill with water, and you feel the pain of suffocation, wondering why you are dying, until you lose consciousness at last.

The defendant, James Ford Seale, was responsible for this. He hadn't expected these two young men ever to be seen again, but parts of them drifted to the surface. The law searched and found even more of them, a skull and ribs. But time marched on, and Henry and Charles were forgotten, until the government made a deal with the devil, Charles Marcus Edwards, who was given an ultimatum: tell the truth and go free, or lie and go to jail. He finally told the truth. Believe the story because other facts tie in with it, like the search of the church. If you want to know whom to blame for justice taking this long to find a home, it was Sheriff Hutto and the highway patrolman: if they had told the FBI about the search of the church that morning, the whole case would have blown wide open then and there. You might not like Edwards walking away a free man— we don't like it either—but it's the only way to get whatever justice is left.

Lampton pauses, collects his notes, and walks slowly, carefully, as if not to disturb the images, to his seat at the prosecution table.

Powerful, maybe a little overdone, but designed to keep hold of the jurors' hearts and minds during Nester's argument, until Fitzgerald can come on stage and finish the story with a dagger's thrust.

Nester goes straight at her quarry; she needs to show him not as a stumbling bull who found himself in the ring and didn't quite know how to get out but as the bull who convinces you to watch his feet and not his horns as he pounds across the ring. This entire case is based on one man's memory, she stresses, one man's story of what happened forty-three years ago; without it, there is nothing.

This man, an admitted liar many times over, told Connie Chung "from the bottom of his heart" that he had nothing to do with the murder of Dee and Moore, just like he told you, the jury, "from the bottom of his heart," that Seale's story was the truth. Why in the world would anyone believe his latest version? If the government is so sure of the truth, why didn't it polygraph the new story, the one in which Seale confesses to Edwards? And why would Seale confess anyway? He and Edwards weren't friends. Edwards didn't even know the place or time of day, only the facts that would nail Seale and get himself out of the ring, keep him out of jail and his family safe.

Without him, there is nothing. Nothing.

Pastor Briggs's famous journal doesn't even mention Edwards or Seale. Edwards tells you a story he denied knowing only days before. He lied after he was given immunity, for God's sake. He couldn't stop lying. Taken to a room and strapped to a machine, he suddenly came up with a story: Yes, now I remember. Now I remember. James Seale told me all about it. Funny how Edwards just happened to remember the necessary elements of the case: that the car crossed states lines and that the victims were alive. Don't you think they might have suffocated in the trunk after all those hours? There is no credible evidence as to how they died. There's no credible evidence as to anything in this case.

Then Nester addresses, as she must, the *Mississippi Burning* problem—all the "reign of terror" Klan evidence intended to allow the jury to right the wrongs of the white man against the black man, to convince the world that Mississippi has overcome, or is overcoming, or is at least trying to overcome its painful, racist past. You can't undo the harm of the past, she insists, you can't seek justice for the state, here, in this courtroom, because my client is entitled to justice on his own. Everyone is entitled to justice on his own, even those who offend us. You can't convict Seale for the sake of the state's reputation, for being a member of the Klan. To make everyone feel better.

Looking the jury directly in the eye, Nester finishes on her strongest point: you simply cannot convict on a liar's word.

Her passion is powerful, and as the jury watches her walk from the podium to the defense table, it seems, for the moment at least, convincing. The government here is a runaway train, and you should worry because some day it might be speeding down the track at you.

Fitzgerald waits until Nester has returned to her seat, then picks up her notes and steps to the podium. She faces the jurors.

"One man's word?" she asks incredulously. "Remember the words of James Ford Seale: 'Yes, but I'm not going to admit it. You're going to have to prove it.'"

She swings and points at Seale—she needs to paint a mask of violence on this dilapidated face—and declares him unrepentant and arrogant, confident through the years that no one would ever talk, that the silent bones, the skull without a jaw or four front teeth, the ribs, would rest on the bottom of the river forever. This trial is the story of the journey of these bones from the river bed to this courtroom.

The evidence is good beyond a reasonable doubt: the evidence corroborates Seale's story; it corroborates Edwards's story. As for Edwards, yes, *he is a liar and a killer*; he planned the kidnapping and conspired with the others to kill the boys. He's as guilty as Seale, and you can be repulsed by him and judge him, but you can do all that and still believe him. He is believable: he didn't minimize his own role, and its very terribleness shows the terrible truth.

Edwards acknowledged to his congregation what he had done, which is not the action of a lying man. Why would he make this story up? The truth was submerged. The truth kicked itself free of the chains of fear and hatred. Seale drowned Charles Moore and Henry Dee, but he did not drown the truth.

Fitzgerald remains still at the podium for several seconds while silence envelops the room. She has brought righteousness and reason together. There is only one way to release the present from the grip of the terrible past: find James Ford Seale guilty of the crimes charged.

Wingate-as-Moses further instructs the jury. As they file obediently out of the jury box, the room is so quiet you can hear the shuffle of the jurors' feet. Now, the waiting. Some in the audience exchange phone numbers and leave. Others linger in the hallway, suspecting the jury might be back within the hour.

The final scene is at hand; the chorus is deliberating on the defendant's fate. When it returns with a judgment, the curtain will fall. James Ford Seale will either live out his remaining days in freedom or die in prison. Mississippi will have taken another step on the long path toward resolving its past, or, in the eyes of the world anyway, it will have stumbled backwards.

CHAPTER 37

Jury trials are always a roll of the dice, which is why guilty people often choose them. There are no valid predictors about jury behavior, but a quick verdict is usually a bad sign for the defense: the jury didn't have to think too hard to nail the defendant. This jury is back in two hours. The speed of the verdict reinvigorates the sense that this trial has been more like a play, scripted from start to finish, with the end certain before the curtain rose.

Not everyone anticipates a guilty verdict. L. C. Dorsey has been convinced of Seale's guilt from the first moment, yet still doesn't believe he will go to prison. The past is too much present in her. Even after living for several years in Massachusetts and Washington, D.C., and becoming a tenured faculty member at Mississippi State College, she still can't bring herself to ride alone in a car with a white man in the Delta.

Burl Jones is nervous. He can't overcome his sense of amazement that the trial is taking place at all. There's a God somewhere, he thinks. There has to be for Mississippi to change like this.

All seats are filled. Suddenly, the courtroom falls quiet, as if a bell has signaled the moment, and in the air, under the bright lights, one feels a palpable sympathy for the small, elderly man at the defense table, who in his silence and ill health seems so remote from whatever he might have been or done forty-three years before and whose fate is now in the hands of twelve strangers. The moment passes as suddenly as it came, like a broken leaf lifted from the ground by a sudden gust. The memory of the crime itself sweeps in and settles the air.

Seale is not wearing the usual hearing device. He sits motionless, with his hand on his mouth, as juror number four stands and hands the ballot to the marshal, who takes it to the judge. Wingate reviews it, then passes it to the clerk, who reads it aloud.

As to count one, kidnapping of Charles Moore: guilty.

As to count two, kidnapping of Henry Dee: guilty.

As to count three, conspiracy: guilty.

Burl Jones murmurs a harsh "Yes!" with each guilty and pumps his fist in front of him. Behind him, a female voice says, "Thank you, Jesus!" Thelma Collins weeps. Seale and his two lawyers sit motionless.

The judge commands Seale to rise and step forward. Nester and Lucas hold him by the arms and walk him to the podium. An expressionless Thomas Moore tracks his movement. Oddly, the judge explains that as a convicted felon, Seale cannot now possess a gun, even for display or hunting.

Seale wobbles back to his seat, looking at his wife through fragile frames: "Are you okay? Are you okay?" he asks her. She nods. He gives Nester a hug and little kiss on the cheek.

Energy is wild at the prosecution table. Fitzgerald's color has risen to a bright red. Lampton is grinning widely as he packs up his briefcase. Eight up and eight down for Mississippi now. Altogether, twenty-six convictions for the South. The train that Mississippi stoked up seventeen years ago with the prosecution and conviction of Byron De La Beckwith rolls onward.

Outside, on the courthouse steps, Thomas Moore and Thelma Collins face the media. "After all these years," Collins says, still in tears, "I never thought this day would come." Moore expresses in his firm voice his new feelings toward Mississippi. "I want the world to know that Mississippi spoke tonight. The jury is from Mississippi, and I hope that every citizen of Mississippi and Franklin County can rest tonight with the veil of shame off their eyes. I now feel that Mississippi is my home, something I wouldn't have owned up even as of last night." Thomas imagines walking along with his brother and friend Henry Dee in heaven, rejoicing at the justice that finally came.

Dorsey cannot hate James Ford Seale or the others. For one thing, she could never in her mind quite put Seale on the bank of the river with the two boys; for another, she remembers well how, growing up, the teachings of her church had prevented her fear of whites from turning into hate. I am powerless, you are powerful, but I will not hate you. Anger, yes, a little, but it had faded with the passage of time. She obtained her master's degree in social work from the State University of New York in Stony Brook where two male Jewish professors had tutored her at night and on weekends, on their own time—she brought back to Mississippi a taste for lox and bagels—in methods of research and writing and also edited her papers. For the first time, she had felt like a person in a white man's eyes, and it was there that she learned how to walk in another person's shoes. She feels guilt, and always will, on behalf of the black community for failing to protect those two boys, for failing to protect Emmett Till.

For Dorsey, the trial had heightened the sensation of those times and left her unsettled. In a downtown deli the day after the verdict, she is upset when a white waitress treats her rudely—until she sees the waitress act just as rudely, if not more so, toward a white customer. How it lingers in us older ones, she thinks. We're still trapped in the fear and the pain of our past. For our grandchildren, it will be different. Her grandson will not be afraid to pass a white man on the sidewalk or sit next to him in a bar. He won't have to fear white people showing up at the door. He can let them come in.

Jim Ingram, who worked the case as a young FBI agent in 1964 and came out of retirement in 2006 to work it a second time, has never wavered in his belief that Seale is a killer. The word that comes to mind on hearing the jury pronounce the verdict is "finally." After all this time, justice has finally caught up with James Ford Seale.

Up to the end, Nester thought she had a shot. In truth, she realizes afterward, the verdict had been a foregone conclusion. The end of the script was written in the very beginning, when the jurors filled out questionnaires about their feelings toward the violent history of the Ku Klux Klan and the movies *Mississippi Burning* and *Ghosts of Mississippi*. She could have danced naked on a tabletop, and it wouldn't have made a difference. Her husband, a nonlawyer, had it right when he said that juries look for good guys and bad guys. If they decide the defendant is a bad guy, he's a dead man, regardless of the evidence. This jury decided Seale was a bad guy.

Saturday morning, June 16, arrives bright and hot in Meadville. Around 9 A.M. TV trucks and reporters begin gathering at what had been in 1964 the ice cream stand on the edge of town. Movement people, observers, and a few local blacks mix in with the media. Across the street, Thomas Moore begins digging a hole in the ground at the exact spot where he believes his brother and Henry Dee were standing when Seale stopped for them. (David Ridgen is filming his every move for the documentary, even sticking the snout of his camera into the hole.) Moore had earlier planted a memorial to his brother and Henry in this spot, but it had been ripped out. Today, he is planting a new one in cement. Wearing a black hat embossed with "U.S. Army" in large gold letters, tan pants, a B. B. King T-shirt, and fingerless gloves, he twists the posthole digger deeper and deeper into the ground, beginning to work up a sweat. With him are his son, Thelma Collins, numerous cousins, and several preachers. Thelma is holding a small American flag. Thomas, the rock, the warrior, pauses to wipe the sweat from his brow. A friend empties half a bag of cement into the hole, TV cameras whirring at the sight. Thomas pours water from a plastic jug into the hole and with a stick swirls the mixture. He sinks a pole attached to a black metal oval sign into the cement and holds it steady. The sign says in white lettering,

In Memory of
Henry Hezekiah Dee
&

Charles Eddie Moore
Abducted and Killed by the Klan
2 May 1964
Bodies Found in Mississippi River
July 12th and 13th 1964

A piece of dark, polished wood has been screwed to the pole beneath the sign. Attached to the wood, encased in plastic, are photos of Charles and Henry, the same ones used in the trial. Thomas carefully attaches two American flags to the pole, one at the top, so when the wind blows the red and white stripes ruffle over the boys' names, and one further down, so the stars shine beneath the boys' faces. On this spot, close to this day, at this time of year, at this hour, the boys had stood.

For a moment, the power of their innocence expands into the ions in the damp air, into the woods beyond, and almost unbearably into your heart. It becomes difficult to breathe. A minister in a suit and tie steps forward and leads the crowd in a gospel song. Everyone but you seems to know the words, but it doesn't matter. You raise your hands and clap along in time as the song gathers steam. Prayers are given, honoring the young men, honoring God and his Son. Traffic moves slowly on the road behind the group. A sheriff's car slows down. A young black deputy at the wheel raises his hand to Burl Jones, who waves back.

Thomas Moore and Thelma Collins each say a few words. Moore pitches hard for a bill, inching through

Congress, that will set aside a chunk of money for prosecuting old civil rights crimes similar to this one. "The U.S. government owes every citizen the right to find out what happened to their loved ones." Edwards, he says, after a pause, Edwards was as guilty as Seale, but they had to have his testimony.

Moore has one final stop before he leaves Mississippi: the cemetery. He needs to talk to his brother; he needs to say that he made him a promise to bring him justice, and at 6:30 on the evening of June 14, 2007, that promise was kept. "Mississippi, I'm so proud of you. The veil of shame is off your eyes."

On the same day, in the afternoon, Barack Obama comes to Jackson for a private fund-raiser. He stops by Peaches Café on Farish Street, the cultural and economic center of the black community in Jim Crow days and now, with some exceptions, a street of abandoned buildings. Battling Hillary Clinton for the Democratic nomination, he is not yet a huge star; his entourage consists of a couple of limousines, the Secret Service, and several police cars. Twenty or so members of the media have joined a small group of onlookers on the sidewalk. Obama, in white shirt and silver tie, bounds out of a limousine and waves briefly to the small gathering before disappearing inside, where a crowd of thirty or forty awaits him. He speaks with several of the locals, including a shoe repairman who has worked in a shop next door for sixty years. He poses for pictures and signs autographs. He sings a few bars of "Misty Blue" with a local blues artist. Someone hands him a paper bag with a piece of peach cobbler inside. Then it's time to leave.

Outside, Obama smiles and waves to the crowd. He talks for a few moments about energizing the minority community. He thanks the few who are there, waves good-bye, and slips back into his limousine. The cars speed away for the fund-raiser at the Mississippi TeleCom Center.

When asked that day why he is visiting Mississippi, Obama replies, "People in Mississippi have the same concerns as people in other states, whether it's the lack of health care, or they can't afford to send their children to college, or jobs." Mississippi, in other words, is like any other place in America.

CHAPTER 38

Fittingly, a memorial service for the three civil rights workers is held the next day at the Mount Zion Methodist Church in Longdale, Neshoba County. The three were murdered on June 20, 1964, Father's Day, and the church holds the service every year on Father's Day, which this year falls on June 17. Fannie Lee Chaney, James Chaney's mother, who died a few weeks earlier, is being remembered as well this year.

Jewell McDonald, whose brother and mother were beaten badly the night the church was burned, helps organize the service every year. In 2005, the service was held during the middle of the Killen trial; the jury convicted Edgar Ray the Tuesday after Father's Day. Rita Schwerner Bender, widow of Michael Schwerner, was in town for the trial and spoke at the service that afternoon.

Usually at least three hundred people jam into the small church: victims' family members, the media, members of other churches, people from nearby communities. It's hot this time of year, and volunteers pass out bottles of water during the service, which usually runs close to three hours, way too long in McDonald's mind.

This year the service is more elaborate than usual, but less elaborate than the one held on the twenty-fifth anniversary of the killings. The gathering has the tone of neither a funeral nor a celebration. They're remembering the sacrifice of the "three young men," as she calls them. Songs are sung, scriptures are read, and a guest speaker talks about the tribulations of the past, the changes that have occurred, and the hopes for the future.

During the service, McDonald is so busy running around taking care of things that she hears little of the ceremony. She pauses, however, to join in the song sung every year with great passion: "Lift Every Voice and Sing," known as the Negro National Anthem.

People in the church and in the community are aware that five men allegedly involved in the killing are still alive and walking free. Jewell McDonald and others on the Philadelphia Coalition intend to issue a new statement calling for additional prosecutions in the murder of the three young men.

There are no harsh words inside the church, no recriminations or demands or finger pointing, although McDonald and a good many others in the black community believe that some local blacks cooperated with the white men on the night of the church burning. Those feelings linger, but they do not dominate. The past is something to understand, to honor, and to move on from.

CHAPTER 39

The sentencing hearing for James Ford Seale on August 25 turns into a reunion of sorts. Many of those from the trial show up for the final scene. Today, Wingate will pronounce judgment. Seale sits at the table, wrists and ankles shackled, wearing an orange jumpsuit with Madison County Jail stenciled in black letters on the back. His ever-loyal wife and her daughter and son-in-law sit grimly on the bench behind him.

Otherwise, there's an almost festive air to the gathering, as if it were a grand finale or curtain call. The absence of the jury lessens the need for propriety. Chatter rises and falls, interrupted by bursts of friendly laughter. Until the judge appears, when all stand and fall quiet. The penalty ranges from one year to life on each count, and no one doubts Seale will receive the maximum. But it is important to hear the words from on high. It is important for Thomas Moore, on his own path to redemption, to speak directly to his brother's murderer. For everyone to see James Ford Seale clink and rattle away through the door one last time.

Fitzgerald flourishes the dagger. Flush, proud, elegant as usual, she allows her passion to flare as she describes Seale as "inhuman, monstrous, barbaric," and lacking a "shred of compassion or human decency." She stresses that Seale has had "forty-three years of freedom to enjoy the sweetness of life since he stripped Charles Moore and Henry Dee of theirs." Whatever days he has left should be spent in prison.

Thomas Moore approaches the podium with paper in hand. He reads from it slowly, his hands grasping the podium, head lowered. He tells of how the snuffing out of the dream of his brother's life left him an untrusting person who pushed people away, of how he has cried whenever he imagines Charles and Henry's suffering at Seale's hands or the thoughts in their minds during their last few moments of consciousness, of how he has wondered if Charles cried out for him at the end. Suddenly, he turns to Seale, shakes the papers in his face, says, "Look at you now, with your sick ego. Look at you now." Seale stares at a spot on the wall behind the judge as Moore lays a strange curse on him. "I hope the spirits of Charles and Henry come to your cell every night and visit with you to teach you what is meant by love of your fellow man."

Glancing at Seale, Moore tells movingly of his own redemption: "On June 14th 2007, the day you were convicted, I started the healing process and moving on with my life. In a few hours I will walk away from here leaving the chains of pain, guilt, hate, and shame that have hung over me the past forty-three years."

Thomas Moore's most profound hope is that "Charles and Henry will be able to finally rest in peace, 'Anywhere in Glory,' as it says on Charles's gravestone." He softens the pain in the courtroom a little by describing a vivid, happy scene: "I hope the three of us, one day, will gather around the throne of God and continue our friendship and love that was taken away by the evil action of you and your fellow Ku Klux Klansmen."

Thelma Collins speaks for herself and two sisters, who stand silently on either side of her at the podium. She tells the judge that they were deeply offended by Seale's mocking gestures during the trial, his laughing and thumbs up signals to his wife, his total lack of remorse. As for herself, she's hurt so badly over the years that she's had to see a psychiatrist. She's glad justice has been done, and she thanks the people who've worked so hard for it.

Nester knows that nothing she says will make a difference in what happens. But she explains to the court and the victims' families that in his gestures, Seale had been referring only to his medical condition: thumbs up to his wife meant only that he was feeling better. He meant no disrespect. In a plea for Seale to be sent to a medical facility, Nester lists his many maladies and argues that although he won't last long under any conditions, he's entitled to decent medical care. It's important to remember, she mentions in the course of her presentation, that the defendant still claims his innocence. In all these years, he's been a model citizen.

This insistence on innocence makes the final scene easier: Seale is not asking for forgiveness; he is not seeking redemption. He is the same man he was in 1964. He deserves what he's going to get this day. When Wingate asks him if he wishes to make a statement, Seale rises, says no softly, and sits back down. The judge explains that he has received two letters on Seale's behalf, one from his step-daughter, sitting behind him, who writes that he's a good man.

It's time for Wingate to slip out of the role of God's lawgiver and even-handed administrator of justice and make his feelings known. In his deliberate, mellow baritone, the judge proclaims that although the crime is forty-three years old, "justice is ageless." And he notes that "the pulse of the community throbs with sorrow." He says these words with a surprising lack of feeling in his voice, as if he's saying what he's expected to say. "The crime is so horrific, so unspeakable," he continues, "that only a monster could have done it." The judge understands that Seale is a good family man and that he hasn't gotten into trouble all these years, but the ghastly nature of the crime requires that he impose three life sentences. He will recommend, at the defense's request, placement of the defendant in a medical facility. Nester's motion to have her ill client released on bail pending appeal is denied.

"All rise!"

Wingate exits through the door behind him. Seale stands unsteadily, smiles at his wife, and clinks slowly across the room. Nester huddles with the family. People stand hesitantly, looking about. The lack of passion, or perhaps satisfaction, in the judge's voice, in his demeanor, hangs in the air for a moment.

The curtain falls. After a few moments of darkness, the lights go up.

CHAPTER 40

In the town of Sumner in late August 2007, Jerome Little, organizer of the Emmett Till Commission, has a serious problem. The ceremony and press conference are set for October 2, and he still doesn't have a proclamation from the commission. Every member must sign the statement, without a single holdout, or the meaning of the whole event is lost. Everything comes down to a few words.

The dispute has been brewing for almost a year. Susan Glisson, director of the William Winter Institute for Racial Reconciliation, brought a draft proclamation to the table last summer, and it was to be read aloud and put up for a vote. After reading it, Frank Mitchener, the wealthy plantation owner, announced that he wasn't going to sign the document and walked out of the room. Jerome Little freaked out, and white cochair Betty Pearson rushed to contact Mitchener at home before the meeting broke up.

Mitchener was clear: the document stated that the signers, on behalf of the community, apologized for the death of the young boy, which Mitchener felt he could not do. To apologize would be to admit that he was involved in the horrible murder of this black boy, and he wasn't. He wouldn't say it.

Pearson reasoned with him: Frank, it doesn't actually say you did it, that you were responsible for it. It's just a word. Don't let's get hung up on it. Mitchener was adamant: he would not sign. He couldn't be sorrier for what had happened to that boy, but he had nothing to do with it.

Little saw the whole project slipping away. The more he thought about it, the actual wording wasn't that important; what was important was that the process continue, that this black-and-white effort succeed. A PR person from Chicago, Jessie Jaynes, had joined the team and got the word about the ceremony out to the national media. There were even rumors that Barack Obama might attend. The Till family was onboard; Little had arranged for the sheriff's department to provide a formal escort for them from Clarksdale to Sumner. The governor himself might be there. Little decided he didn't care what the document said—he told Pearson that it could read "meow, meow, meow" for all he cared—as long as every member of the commission signed it. Including Frank Mitchener.

Glisson had made the wording of the proclamation as strong as possible with the idea that the language could be amended or toned down in negotiations. A struggle over the wording could be a good thing. After the meltdown over the Jesse Jackson/Al Sharpton incident, she had spent the next day on the phone reassuring the commission members that this sort of thing would test the commission and bring it out stronger on the other side. And it had. Every incident built a little more trust.

But Frank Mitchener had left the room, and he needed to be brought back in. Time was passing. At Pearson's suggestion, Glisson met with Mitchener at his house. She listened to his position and did not argue. Instead, she explained that in the eyes of the world, two guilty men had been acquitted of the murder of Emmett Till in this community and that the community, by its silence, had acquiesced in the tragedy. She didn't think the town had acquiesced, but until it spoke up and said otherwise, that was how it would look. With that image, the town would stagnate; development would never come.

Mitchener listened thoughtfully. Glisson left him a copy of the proclamation and asked him to make whatever changes were necessary to satisfy him. After some hesitation, he agreed.

Little kept the pressure on the plantation owner as well. He called Mitchener, went to his house, urged, asked, finagled, and demanded. One more week, Little said, and then we're going on without you. But he couldn't, and Mitchener knew he couldn't. Mitchener was determined not to be rushed, believing that deliberation yielded the best results.

In early September, Mitchener made his changes. "Apology" was gone. "Regret" and "sorry" were in. Now the proclamation read that the community expressed "deep regret" for the "failure to effectively pursue justice" and stated, "We wish to say to the family of Emmett Till that we are profoundly sorry for what was done in this community to your loved one." Mitchener gave the amended document to Glisson, who voiced no objection.

Little looked up the words "apology" and "regret" in the dictionary. They seemed to mean the same thing. He checked with the Till family. They agreed that the words meant essentially the same thing and signed off on the proclamation as amended. Frank Mitchener brought the document to the next meeting, read it aloud, and moved for its adoption. Without discussion, the commission unanimously approved the proclamation.

The deal was done; everybody was back at the table. Another thread of trust was now wound in and around the members of the commission, drawing them closer together.

CHAPTER 41

Sumner is about sixteen miles southeast of Clarksdale, the home of William Handy, the father of the blues, on Highway 49, recently renamed the Emmett Till Memorial Highway. You turn off the highway at a white wooden marker, pass through a residential area, and come to a small rise and a set of railroad tracks. If you go straight for a few blocks, you reach a bridge spanning a wide bayou. On the right is the courthouse, a gray-brown Romanesque building built in 1905 with arches rather than pillars and an imposing four-story clock tower. Many of the storefronts around the square are empty, although three lawyer's offices and two pharmacies have survived. There are no grocery stores or cafes. On top of a flagpole in front of the cathedral-like building flies the American flag, and beneath it flies the Mississippi flag, the Stars and Bars rippling out in the slightest breeze. On the corner to the east stands a marble statue of a Confederate soldier. In one hand he holds a rifle; the other is raised to his brow as he gazes over the horizon. At his feet are carved the words

Our Heroes
1861–1865

A poem by Virginia F. Boyle, known as the poet laureate of the Confederacy, is carved on the column beneath the soldier.

For truth dies
Not and by her
Light they raise
The flag whose
Starry folds have
Never trailed
And by the low
Tents of the
Deathless dead
They lift the
Cause that never
Yet has failed

At each of the four corners of the base of the column is placed a stone cannonball. On the base itself is inscribed:

To the Tallahatchie
Rifles and All Who Served
From This County.
Erected by the Daughters of the Confederacy 1913.

On the west corner of the courthouse, a few yards away, stands the newly planted Emmett Till memorial sign, donated by Morgan Freeman's foundation, now draped in red velvet, to be revealed at the conclusion of the ceremony.

On the morning of October 2, 2007, in front of the courthouse, the scene is bustling; workers have been up since dawn constructing the dais, now decked out in red, white, and blue bunting, and laying out row after row of chairs. Jessie Jaynes has set up a table stacked with press kits. A medical tent has been erected off to the side. School buses from surrounding towns and one from as far away as Birmingham, Alabama, roll in, park across the street, and unload gaggles of students. Supervisors Jerome Little and Bobby Banks, in summer suits and ties, oversee the execution of the details.

Suddenly, over the railroad tracks, appears a Tallahatchie County sheriff's car, then another, and another, all with black deputies at the wheels. The cars stop at the side entrance of the courthouse. Members of the Till family, including Simeon Wright and Wheeler Parker, get out and glance around for a moment at the pageantry. They head inside the building to join other dignitaries for coffee and doughnuts before the ceremony.

The day promises to be hot. Seats for the elderly are in the shade, next to boxes of water bottles. The ceremony begins on time. The master of ceremonies is black state senator and president of the Greenville city council David Jordan. Standing in front of a podium bearing the seal of the Tallahatchie County Board of Supervisors, Jordan begins by remarking on how different things are now in Mississippi from fifty-two years ago. Look at us working together, black and white. The only thing he used to run for was his life! All this change is evidence that there is a just God, because God did it; God decided not to allow ignorance, hatred, or prejudice. Give God credit; you might not know how He did it, but He did.

The audience nods and murmurs its approval of this notion. Jordan goes on with a strange, almost erotic metaphor: Mississippi was like a woman with a fancy dress, but her underclothes were dirty. Now we've cleaned up the underclothes, we're going to wash her off and dress her in black and white.

For the formal invocation of God's presence, a white minister declares that in the name of Jesus Christ, our Lord and Savior, we acknowledge the community's regret for the past injustices.

A female soloist comes to the mike and sings mournfully about how we must pray that we will be ready for His return, gathering loud murmurs of approval from the audience. A glance around reveals a gathering of three to four hundred people, roughly 90 percent of whom are black. Most of the whites are either students from Ole Miss helping Glisson facilitate the event, media, or members of the commission.

Little takes the podium and describes the long road the commission has traveled and the growing pains it has suffered along the way. He joins in the belief that God has brought them to this point. Mississippi has some ghosts that are now out of the closet, and he says to the family of Emmett Till, "We regret that this happened. We're sorry that it happened."

Bobby Banks, the other black county supervisor, is not so careful with his choice of words: he declares, "We want to apologize to the family. We're sorry for what happened, and it's time to apologize." The white sheriff of Tallahatchie resembles the stereotype of the southern sheriff— short with a large gut and stubby arms—but he doesn't talk like one. "We apologize for what happened," he says. "I can't imagine what it must have been like to go through it." And although he regrets the crime, he himself had nothing to do with it; he was just a dream in his mommy's and daddy's hearts when Emmett Till was murdered. Personally, he doesn't care if someone is pink, blue, black, or white—he treats everyone the same. (This is not an uncommon declaration by whites in Mississippi of their lack of racial prejudice.)

Standing to the side of the crowd, arms folded, badges glinting in the mid-morning sun, are the young black sheriffs of surrounding Leflore and Sunflower counties. A middle-aged black woman with streaks of gray in her hair approaches them, introduces herself, and says that she was a member of "SNICK" in the old days.

"What's that?" one of them asks politely.

"Student Nonviolent Coordinating Committee," she says. "You've never heard of it?"

"No, ma'am."

"Really? I can't believe it."

The Till family takes the stage. Simeon Wright, the Mississippi cousin, now from Chicago, recalls that he watched part of the trial in 1955 and was perhaps the only person in the courtroom who thought Milam and Bryant were going to be convicted. He chastises Leflore County, where Emmett was actually kidnapped and murdered, for not coming forward like Tallahatchie. "I accept your apology," he says. "There was no one to help in 1955 when Emmett was murdered, but you are doing it today, and tomorrow. Thank you."

Another cousin, Debra Watts, says for the first time in her life, "It's good to be in Mississippi. The world has been holding its breath for fifty-two years and now it's exhaling and bringing a new day of hope. We accept your apology, on behalf of the family. And your regrets."

Wheeler Parker, the Chicago cousin who traveled to Mississippi with Emmett and is now a minister, recounts how he and Emmett had been warned by relatives that they couldn't behave down in Mississippi the way they did in Chicago because there would be no one to help them. And when they did, there wasn't. The men came into the bedroom looking for Emmett with a pistol and a flashlight, and Wheeler was shaking like a leaf and prayed only that he would be allowed to live.

"God is in control," he says.

"Amen," says the crowd back.

"God is in control!"

"Emmett Till spoke louder in death than he would have if he had lived. Like Cain and Abel, Emmett's blood cries out from the ground."

Commission cochairs Betty Pearson and Robert Grayson, mayor of Tutwiller, who grew up picking cotton on Pearson's father's plantation, take the podium and read the official proclamation of regret and sorrow for the injustice committed. Members of the commission—other than Mitchener, who had a church obligation—take the stage to loud applause, and their picture is taken. Pearson apologizes to Simeon Wright for what was done to his cousin and hands him the proclamation.

Jordan introduces former governor William Winter (1980–1984) as the "greatest governor since Reconstruction." He states that Mississippi, the entire state, "deplores and apologizes" for what happened fifty-two years ago, and then he looks to the future. The best way to honor

Emmett Till's memory is to move forward on getting decent education and jobs for blacks, to ensure that all are safe in the streets and in their homes and are treated with dignity and respect. All of us are children of God.

Amen.

The day has grown hot; the kids are restless. Another song is sung. God can wipe away your tears. He cares for you. He'll come down. The crowd moves over to the memorial sign. Little carefully pulls a gold rope, and the velvet drape opens to reveal a green metal sign trimmed in white with a white magnolia blossom perched on top. Raised gold lettering briefly tells the story of Emmett Till's murder and the trial. The crowd claps while looking up at the sign and reading the words.

Organizers have arranged for buses to take the visitors on a driving tour of the crime sites. Volunteers hand out brochures entitled "Tallahatchie Civil Rights Driving Tour." Signs similar to the one on the courthouse lawn, although not yet finished, are being made for each of the sites. Three buses, escorted by four sheriff's cars, set out across the back roads of the Delta, through tiny dilapidated towns, past fields of harvested cotton and corn, in search of the story.

The buses stop at what's left of the funeral parlor in Tutwiler, where Emmett's body was embalmed and prepared for shipment to Chicago, a process it's said took over sixteen hours. The buses travel to the Glendora cotton gin, where Milam and Bryant, after having tortured (for three hours) and murdered Till, stopped to get a seventy-five-pound gin fan, which they attached to the body with barbed wire before dumping it in the Tallahatchie River. Then to the Bryant Grocery and Meat Market in Money, where Carolyn Bryant was working when she claimed Emmett grabbed her hand and asked her for a date and outside which Simeon Wright and others say Emmett wolf-whistled at her. Although the market's fragile wooden remains look like they could tumble down in a hard wind, its owner recently offered to sell the building to the state for $4 million for a museum. Finally, the tour buses turn down a wandering dirt road to the spot where Emmett's body was thought to have been dragged from the river.

At each spot, a narrator recounts the facts. Simeon Wright stands in front of the store to tell the crowd of what he saw and heard here; at the river, Plater Robinson, of the Southern Institute for Education and Research at Tulane University, considered by many to be the foremost authority on the case, tells of the fisherman who spotted the foot sticking up out of the water. The buses load up, the sheriff's cars lead off, and the entourage swirls clouds of dust as it rolls down the road to the next site.

You soon realize, as you listen, that almost every fact of the story is in dispute: where the fan came from, where the body was pulled from the river, who was in the truck carrying Emmett Till from the house, who shot him, how many blacks were involved. Different people hold different narratives close to their hearts. Simeon Wright is adamant that he and the others at the store that fatal day did not egg Emmett into doing whatever it was he did, although both Wright and Parker Wheeler admit that Emmett did in fact wolf-whistle at Bryant. The black mayor of Webb insists that his father was involved in the incident, although others dispute that claim.

As the discussions continue at the sites and on the buses, the trip takes on the feel of a historical adventure, like a guided tour of a Civil War battlefield, with the brutal facts glazed over by the remoteness of time and a neutral recitation. It strikes you at odd moments—staring into the muddy waters of the Tallahatchie, listening and watching as Wright points to the spot outside the grocery where the boys were standing when Emmett whistled—how remarkable it is that this is happening at all, here in Mississippi, and how necessary this reconstruction of the crime into a historical event is for the past to take its proper place, always present but not defining the present or limiting the future.

Eventually, the sheriff's cars and the buses find their way back to the school in Sumner, where a light buffet is served. Discussions continue, phone numbers are exchanged, and some of the remaining figures in the story pose for pictures with visitors.

Looking back on it, Jerome Little has only one regret: that he didn't get to see the sheriff's cars carrying the Till family into town. When he first ran for county supervisor in the seventies, he lost by a few hundred votes, and on election night, he was driving across those tracks and by the courthouse when a white man called out to him, "Go on home, nigger Little. You lost."

Little sat up straight. "Yeah," he replied, "but I'll be back. I'll be back." And he had come back, and he had wanted so badly to see those sheriff's cars coming across the tracks, like he had on that night years ago. He gets tears in his eyes talking about the commission and the ceremony—whites and blacks sitting across from each other at the table and working things out, hanging in when things got rough, treating each other with respect, wanting different things but coming together on common ground. He has no illusions: White people want what they want, and so do blacks. They might not be the same things, but it's going to be a little easier for people to get what they want after today because the past is finally out in the open, and some trust has been built up on both sides. It doesn't bother him a bit that most of the white residents of Sumner didn't come to the ceremony. Truthfully, he hadn't expected it.

CHAPTER 42

Perhaps the most heralded use of the word "apology" in Mississippi civil rights history is in regard to the statement made by Secretary of State Richard Molpus in 1989, the twenty-fifth anniversary of the slaying of the three civil rights activists. Molpus said, "We deeply regret what happened here twenty-five years ago. We wish we could undo it. We are profoundly sorry they are gone. We wish we could bring them back." The *New York Times* describes these two sentences as an apology. His statement is almost universally referred to in the media as an apology.

Likewise, most news sources covering the Sumner event stated that the community gave an apology to the Till family. The AP wire headlined, "Tallahatchie leaders officially apologize for Emmett Till's murder, trial." The *Atlanta Journal-Constitution* describes the document read in front of the courthouse as an "official apology." The *Miami Herald* refers to the proclamation as an "apology."

Merriam-Webster defines "regret" as "to be very sorry for." An "apology" is defined as an "admission of error or discourtesy" or an "admission of guilt or fault." It is this latter meaning of the word that so bothers Mitchener and

many other white Mississippians. As one white businessman put it, you can be sorry the Holocaust happened
without apologizing for it. Although you regret the racial
sins of Mississippi's past, you don't apologize for them.

Stanley Dearman, former publisher of the *Neshoba County
Democrat* in Philadelphia and a longtime advocate of civil
rights, argues that every member of a community is responsible for the acts of the entire community; the wealth of
Mississippi was accumulated through the use of slave labor,
and that wealth has been passed down in one form or another to all white Mississippians. Thus, an apology from
white Mississippi is not only appropriate but absolutely necessary for true reconciliation.

Susan Glisson wondered if she would hear from Mitchener about the use of the word "apology" in the papers
after the event. She never did. In fact, the use of the word
didn't bother him. "If that's the way they want to describe
it, it's okay with me." The use of "apology" in the press
didn't bother Mitchener, just as the fact that very few of
the community's white citizens attended the ceremony
didn't bother Little. Mitchener made a successful stand on
an issue that mattered to him, and Little achieved a successful event put together by blacks and whites. Each got
what he wanted.

Meanwhile, as Sumner is busy carrying through on the
promises of the commission, Mitchener is raising money
for the restoration of the courthouse. Costs have risen to
almost $10 million, and the building is now on the Regis-
ter of Historic Places, so care has to be taken to maintain
the original footprint. Little and the county supervisors
received a grant to build an Emmett Till Recreation Cen-

ter for kids on the edge of town. The museum will tell the story of the murder and trial through a collection of articles, photographs, artifacts, and several items belonging to Emmett.

Sumner will continue to celebrate, if not venerate, that which it previously tried to obliterate. The past will exist for a moment in the present of all those who pull off the highway and stop to learn the story of Emmett Till. Even though his murder will most likely remain unavenged, Emmett Till will, if things go as planned, become a source of racial reconciliation in Tallahatchie County and the state of Mississippi. Future historians will note that in 2007 at this courthouse black leaders and white leaders apologized on behalf of the entire community to the family of Emmett Till.

CHAPTER 43

Despite the judge's wishes, Seale was not placed in a medical facility. He was sent, instead, to the federal prison in Terre Haute, Indiana, where his first cell mate was a child molester. On September 9, 2008, a little more than a year after he was sentenced, a guard knocked on his cell door with a message. "Mr. Seale, you're a free man." The guard explained that a newscaster on TV announced that the court had overturned his conviction. As soon as he could get to a phone, Seale called his wife, who confirmed that she had just heard the news of the reversal from the *Clarion-Ledger*'s Jerry Mitchell. Seale would be coming home.

Kathy Nester's argument had won the day: a three-judge panel of the Fifth Circuit Court of Appeals agreed with her that the charges were barred by the statute of limitations. The kidnapping statute originally provided for the death penalty "if the victim had not been liberated unharmed." Another law declared that there is no statute of limitations for capital offenses, which are defined as crimes that carry the death penalty. In 1968 the Supreme Court in *United States v. Jackson* invalidated the death penalty provision in the kidnapping statute because it violated the Fifth and Sixth amendments to the Constitution. In 1972 Congress amended the kidnapping statute to remove the death penalty. That left the kidnapping statute with a five-year statute of limitations.

The Fifth Circuit had to decide whether the 1972 amendments were to be retroactive or prospective; if they were prospective, then the law as it existed in 1964 would continue to apply: the crime would still be considered capital and would therefore have no statute of limitations. But if the amendments were to be applied retroactively, then the kidnapping statute would be considered noncapital as of 1964 and the crime thereby subject to the five-year statute of limitation, which had obviously long since run.

The general rule is that if the overturned or amended statute is considered to be procedural, then the changes will be applied retroactively; if it is considered to be substantive—that is, involving substantive rights—then it will be applied only prospectively.

Statutes of limitations are generally considered to be procedural. For this reason, the court held the amendment should be retroactive. Nester had argued this point before Judge Wingate in a motion filed within days of the indictment in January 2007. Wingate, without much discussion, rejected the argument. Now the Fifth Circuit had overturned his decision.

There was considerable reaction to the reversal. Nester was elated; these charges should never have been brought in the first place, and once brought, Judge Wingate should have dismissed them at the first opportunity. Dunn Lampton and Paige Fitzgerald were terribly disappointed. They had seen the statute-of-limitations problem from the beginning and had taken it to the Solicitor General's Office in the Justice Department, which had approved the filing.

Charles Edwards was upset when he heard the news of the reversal. He had settled into a life of peace and quiet: hunting, fishing, spending time with his family, and occasionally running a 5K or 10K in Natchez or Jackson. He was still scared of Seale and now it seemed Seale would return to the community. He had been laying low for some time, and now he would have to lie even lower. The town of Meadville, Franklin County as a whole, was not happy: with Seale coming back to Roxie, the whole mess would get stirred up again.

The larger community reacted with frustration. All this time and money put into an effort that was reversed not on the merits but on a technicality. Why didn't the judge throw it out in the beginning if the case was no good? Some in the legal community believed that Wingate had clearly seen the statute-of-limitations problem, but the issue was arguable, so he had decided to let the government take its shot and see what happened. A *Jackson Free Press* blogger recounted the story of the law professor who, in response to his students' concern over the law turning on a technicality rather than justice, told them to go outside the building and see whether the words carved in cement over the door said "School of Justice" or "School of Law."

Jeannie Seale was ecstatic. She always knew that James was innocent. He might not be an angel, but he wasn't capable of this sort of crime. On the phone her husband told her not to come up to Indiana to get him; she should stay where she was and he would take the bus down to Jackson.

All he wanted to do when he got home, he told her, was sit and look at her. She laughed, well, then, you'll have a pretty tough job.

Thomas Moore, ever the rock, didn't give up hope: "We're still in the third inning. We've got six more to go." Besides, the whole world knows James Ford Seale is guilty of the crimes. Even if he gets out of prison, justice has been done.

Moore's recently expressed goodwill toward Mississippi apparently doesn't extend to Franklin County. He and Thelma Collins recently filed a civil suit against the county seeking money damages for the crimes against Henry Dee and Charles Moore. Many in the county surmised that the whole thing had been about money from the very beginning.

CHAPTER 44

Not only is the past in Mississippi not dead, it's still seen as the living present, as the way things are today, thanks in large part to *Mississippi Burning*. The movie plays on in the cultural mind of this country like a Jungian myth streaming in the collective unconscious. The great irony is that the movie is not even close to an accurate portrayal of what happened in 1964 in Neshoba County. It's not a movie about the killing of the three civil rights workers; their faces are shown for a total of about thirty seconds, their courage referred to only in passing. It's a movie about two heroic white male FBI agents who come down from the North and manage, through perseverance, ingenuity, and startling brutality, to solve the killings.

Frances McDormand, the wife of the murdering deputy, rats out her husband to Gene Hackman, the cynical, hard-shelled FBI agent who used to be a small-town sheriff in Mississippi, by whispering, as she is kissing him, where the bodies are buried. Blacks, with the exception of a mythical fourteen-year-old boy, are too terrified to assist the FBI, so a black "specialist" is airlifted into the area in a small plane under cover of darkness to break the case. In a makeshift Klan hat, he kidnaps the bigoted loudmouth mayor of the town and takes him to a cabin. There, flashing a razor blade in his face, he threatens to castrate him unless he rats out the murderers, which he does.

Voilà! Case solved. All that's left is for the agents to dress in Klan robes and pretend to lynch a cross-eyed Klansman to get him to give up more names. Hackman's violent and unbalanced character—smiling at inappropriate times, grabbing a Klansman by the balls and twisting—plays well against Willem Dafoe's calm and by-the-book character, until Dafoe, after seeing the results of the beating the murdering deputy had given his wife, and holding a gun to Hackman's head in a fight over how to respond, suddenly agrees to become just as violent, after which, Hackman, under the watchful eyes of Dafoe and other agents, busts up a barbershop with the deputy's head.

Absurdities permeate the film from start to finish, but it is so well acted—Hackman was nominated for best actor for his performance—and the pace is so fast and searing that much is overlooked. As the saying goes, any similarities between the film story and what actually happened in Neshoba County are purely coincidental. Michael Schwerner, one of the two white civil rights workers, is shown driving the car in the chase, and after pulling him over, a Klansman shoots him in the head as he sits behind the wheel. In fact, the evidence shows that James Chaney, the black civil rights worker, was driving and that the Klansmen took all three men from the car before killing them.

In interviews on the CD version, the director, Englishman Alan Parker, attempts to downplay the film's historical inaccuracy by saying that it is fiction, but then he insists that he tried to keep the details as close to the truth as possible. "Burning" is the key for Parker: houses and churches are constantly bursting into flames, to be slowly consumed by raging, leaping licks of fire, and crosses are lit frequently against the night sky, including one outside the FBI agents' motel room. Parker, apparently mesmerized by flaming churches, burns down three of them in the film, even though only one was actually burned at the time.

The real insult to the true narrative, to the civil rights workers themselves, is the fact that the murders themselves were not considered sufficient to carry the story. A good portion of the film consists solely of Hollywood concoctions: a story of the Klan's beating and castrating a black youth for talking to an FBI agent, the hanging of the fourteen-year-old boy's father, apparently for the same sin (in front of a burning barn, of course). Blacks are, for the most part, scared and servile, while the local whites are almost to a person ignorant, thin-lipped yokels who think the three civil rights workers had it coming.

The movie's timeless appeal goes beyond the flames and violence and sex; it lies in the fact that it is a comforting stereotype for the rest of America. That was racism, and it wasn't us, and it still isn't us, and it must still be them. Mississippi is still what it was. We've changed. This Hollywood version of the events in Neshoba County in 1964 ends up being a feel-good movie for the culture at large and a terrible burden for Mississippi to bear in its attempt to reconcile with its past and move on.

CHAPTER 45

Bishop Searcy, the pastor of the New Hope Missionary Baptist Church in Natchez, has his own vision for Mississippi. Searcy grew up in a Natchez full of colored drinking fountains and whites-only swimming pools. He left the state for the seminary, but in 1987 he returned and started a church in an old school house that had been built by a Seale and served as a meeting place for the Klan in the sixties. Although his congregation is mostly black, he dreams of an integrated church. A few whites have joined over the years, but not many stay—their families and friends make life difficult for them. Some black ministers in Natchez have made life difficult for Bishop Searcy, as well, insisting that he's sold out to whites. Searcy is not deterred.

Bishop Searcy preaches empowerment. Blacks have been treated badly for so long that they often just give up. The man with good credit who gets turned down for a house loan says to hell with it, it's never going to change. Bishop Searcy confronts the self-defeating attitude head on, teaching that it's the attitude that's keeping you down today, more than the white man. He wasn't raised to hate whites, but he understands where the bitterness and defeatism come from—a beaten-down people will inevitably point the finger at their oppressor. Blacks need to see what's past as past and deal with the here and now, to move forward in establishing the kingdom on earth, obtaining a transcendence in Christ, without racial division. Too many sacrifices have been made to not continue the progress.

Searcy believes that blacks in Mississippi, churched or unchurched, have a tender heart toward forgiveness. And God's love is like a flowing river; you must remove anything that obstructs the flow of the water, and that includes anger and bitterness.

Searcy also believes that forgiveness—seeking and obtaining it like Charles Edwards did—is an essential step on the path to redemption. To redeem means to buy back that which has been sold. Man was born without sin, but Adam and Eve deprived him of that state of grace through their sins. The wages of sin are death, so death is what is now owed to gain back the original state. The debt can't be paid in gold or silver; it must be paid in blood. But it need not be our blood. Christ shed his blood—the royal blood—to gain our redemption, to pay back what we owed. And it has been done, on the cross. If we accept Christ as our redeemer, we are in fact redeemed. The debt has been paid. We are entitled to eternal life.

In the bishop's view, the price for Mississippi's redemption has been paid. The soil of Mississippi is drenched with the blood of sacrifice—all the soldiers of the Civil War who fell at Corinth and Vicksburg and Champion Hill and Brices Crossroads; all those brilliant minds that were lost, the young boys who died without living. The soil is stained with the blood of white Mississippians who fought for the cause they believed was right—like Paul fighting to persecute the Christians—and with the blood of Mississippi's slaves and the children of slaves and their children who were hung in trees and drowned. The blood of Emmett Till, Medgar Evers, Charles Moore, Henry Dee, Vernon Dahmer, and untold others. The price has been paid. Redemption is here. We need only accept it.

Searcy sees Mississippi as a woman who has lived a rowdy life and now approaches the altar of God, saying, "I'm ashamed of everything that has gone on in my life, and I'm ready to change. I want to change, but I don't know how." Mississippi's soul is walking down the aisle, worn and ragged from her past life, and she's ready to answer God's holy altar call of redemption. She hasn't kneeled down yet, she hasn't received totally the forgiveness of God, but her heart is repentant.

A few miles east of Natchez, the town of Roxie held a celebration of the past and the future. Although 560 people live in town, Roxie has been on a long, downhill slide ever since the sawmill closed in the eighties. Empty buildings are left to collapse; curbs lay broken. People who live here are retired or work in Natchez or Brookhaven. Charles Moore and Henry Dee were headed toward Roxie when Seale stopped to pick them up.

But blacks weren't thinking of James Ford Seale on November 15, 2008. Instead, they were celebrating the fact that one week earlier a black man was elected president of the United States, and they were celebrating the great distance their town and county had come in the past fifty years. Mamie Allen, who left Roxie at age twelve for Chicago with her parents and then returned in the eighties, and Michael Anthony Wright, who was born and raised in Roxie by a black father and a Natchez Indian mother and suspects he might be related to author Richard Wright, conceived the idea the day after the election.

The event was held in what could loosely be called the town park. The railroad used to run through the middle of town. When the tracks were torn up after the mill closed, grass was planted and a covered stage built. Electricity was brought in for sound. Allen and Wright had been frantically putting the logistics of the event together, hustling food, which would all be donated, a sound system, tables, porta-potties, water, programs, speakers, announcements, and fliers. Valencia Dyer, a local children's activist, designed "certificates of participation" to give to kids who attended the celebration. She hung on the front of the stage a banner with a picture of Obama and the slogan "Yes, we can!"

Although blacks in Roxie make up roughly 60 percent of the community, they have never marched on Martin Luther King Jr.'s birthday or had any black celebration in the town park. In Allen's view, it was long past time. There was talk in the community and schools that Obama was really a Muslim and that he wasn't qualified to be president, which was the wrong thing for black kids to be hearing. In her mind, the celebration was for the children of Franklin County. She wanted them to picture a black man in the White House and imagine their own future. She and Michael Wright wanted them to hear the names of the local black heroes and the story of their difficult journeys.

Wright sent an announcement to the *Franklin County Advocate*, still owned by Mary Lou Webb, whose husband had handled publicity for the Americans for the Preservation of the White Race and who had refused to run a story on Seale's indictment for fear of stirring up the past. She ran the announcement next to a note encouraging people to attend community events.

Wright had played football at the local high school, and he remembered that even into the early '80s the white coach restricted blacks to playing certain positions, which did not include quarterback. When a new coach was hired, he decided he wanted the best talent on the field, black or white. Early in the season in 1982, the white quarterback was injured, and a black went in to replace him. Wright still remembers him running onto the field and the shock and consternation on the benches and in the stands when he sat behind center and took the first snap. Last year, it had been a black quarterback who took the Franklin County Bulldogs to the state championship.

The celebration began at 11 A.M. It was unseasonably cold for Mississippi in mid-November, thirty-nine degrees, and the wind was blowing hard under a cloudy sky. Still, around 250 people showed up and gathered around the stage. Only two of the families were white, and they were relative newcomers to town. Tickets for the food were passed out early, and people ate, listened, and socialized as events got under way.

Max Graves, who grew up in Roxie and represented Charles Edwards in the Seale case, attended with his wife. His great-great-grandfather, a plantation owner, had given the land on which they were standing to the town for a

railroad depot and right of way generations ago. Part of
the deal was that the town would be named for his daughter, Roxie. The Graves family did not press a claim to the
land when it reverted due to abandonment by the railroad,
in effect allowing the land to be used as a town park. Max
knew everyone here. He was frustrated that more white
people hadn't shown up.

After Wright introduced the event, preacher Rev. Ricky
O'Quinn gave the invocation and asked for God's blessing
on the day. Bongo drums on stage pounded out African
rhythms. One after another, the speakers took the stage
and marveled at how they never thought they would live to
see the day a black man would occupy the White House
and talked about the hard road their town had taken to get
where it was today. Names of those who had broken barri-
ers were mentioned with pride: first black sheriff, first
black teacher in the integrated schools, first black mayor,
first black election commissioner, first black to work in a
bank, first black veterinarian, and first black cheerleader.
Juanita Brown, a revered member of the community, described vividly the perilous days when she worked as the
first black teacher in the schools.

Mamie Allen invited Max Graves to the stage to speak.
Max is liked in the black community, and he aroused a
good reaction when he admitted that he believed one of
his great-uncles was black. The audience applauded loudly
when he promised to work to bring jobs to Roxie by seeking investors or government grants to open the sawmill.
Now that a black man holds the presidency, he stressed,
such a project might be more feasible.

Toward mid-afternoon, the mic was offered to anyone
who would like to speak. Doris Norman (White George/

Black George) took the stage and described how much racial change had occurred in their community just from the time her first child was born to the time her last child was born. A vendor selling Obama T-shirts and hats from a van on the edge of the park brought an armful of shirts to the stage to be raffled off. Finally, as the air grew even colder and the sky darker, Wright took the stage, thanked everyone for coming, and brought Roxie's first black celebration to a close.

CHAPTER 46

In Mississippi, football comes close to being a religion, with Archie Manning, Brett Favre, Walter Payton, and Jerry Rice its patron saints. The faithful pilgrimage by the tens of thousands to Oxford to watch the Rebels play. Like at Nebraska and Alabama, the game is wrapped in tradition. Many of the traditions here, however, are somewhat suspect to an outside world, which often views any attempt to respect the past in Mississippi as an attempt to honor the racial attitudes of the past. To white Mississippians, you can honor your past and even those who fought and died to protect it without necessarily honoring the values of the culture they fought for.

When Mississippi came under attack in the sixties, the football stadium was the one place it could still shout out its pride—where, on glorious autumn afternoons, it could play "Dixie," wave the Confederate flag, salute its mascot, Colonel Reb, and not feel bad about it. After all, it was during halftime at an Ole Miss football game played in Jackson in the fall of 1962 when Gov. Ross Barnett strode to a microphone at the fifty-yard line and cried into the microphone, "I love Mississippi!" bringing the roar of lions from the crowd. Two days later, the Ole Miss campus erupted in violence and death over the admission of James Meredith to its sacred halls.

The Grove is the site of the largest, and perhaps strangest, tailgating party in the world. Fans stake out hundreds of tents the night before the game, and early the next morning they lay out tables of food and drinks in grand feasts. In some tents, the fans hang crystal chandeliers from the roof and place sterling candelabras on linen tablecloths. Male students in coats and ties and female students in cocktail dresses mingle and sip champagne from crystal flutes until it's time to wander to the bandstand on the edge of the Grove to watch and listen to the band play "Dixie."

The Friday afternoon after Thanksgiving, one of the grandest football traditions in the country takes place, as it has for more than one hundred years: Ole Miss takes on its in-state rival, Mississippi State University, in what is now known as the Egg Bowl. The name derives from the early days of the sport, when the football was blunter and more oval.

This Friday, November 28, 2008, arrives cool, with a promise of rain later in the day. The stadium is near capacity and buzzing with excitement; after four straight losing seasons, Ole Miss is 7 and 4 going into the final game. It has won its last four games, knocking off on the road the last two national champions, Florida 31–30 and LSU 31–13. Kicking LSU's butt at home only six days ago was particularly sweet, and it earned Ole Miss a twentieth ranking in the AP poll. *Sports Illustrated* recently featured Ole Miss on the cover under the headline "Rebels Rise." Days of glory are back, and whipping MSU would not only enhance the rise but make up for last year's humiliating defeat when the Rebels blew a fourteen-point lead in the last few minutes to go down 17–14. It would bring the golden egg home, where it belongs.

In the sixties, Ole Miss wouldn't play teams with black players. It wasn't until the early seventies that Ole Miss successfully recruited a black to the team. Even as the number of black players steadily increased, remnants of the past remained woven into many aspects of the game. The team was, after all, named the Rebels, and the mascot, Colonel Reb, an elderly gentleman with long white hair and a thick bushy mustache, resembled a plantation master who had apparently survived the War of Northern Aggression with only a wound to one leg, which caused him now to lean slightly on a cane. Not long after Colonel Reb's first appearance on the field in 1936, two other primary symbols of southern heritage became a part of Ole Miss football: the Confederate flag and "Dixie."

The Stars and Bars, the battle flag of the Confederacy, were, until a few years ago, to be seen everywhere on the Grove and in the stadium: on the sides of the tents, on the backs of chairs, on the hats and vests of the partiers, on the aerials of their vehicles. Confederate flags were handed out to fans entering the stadium, and bundles of flags were tossed up into the crowds during the game. The crowd stood, the men took off their hats, and flags waved in perfect rhythm when the school band broke into a rousing version of "Dixie," which it did several times a game. The Stars and Bars were indeed the school's flag and "Dixie" its anthem. The band members even wore authentic-looking gray Confederate uniforms and kepi hats.

Oh, I wish I was in the land of cotton,
Old times there are not forgotten,
Look away, look away, look away Dixie Land.

In Dixie Land, where I was born in,
early on one frosty mornin',
Look away, look away, look away Dixie Land.

I wish I was in Dixie, Hooray! Hooray!
In Dixie Land I'll take my stand
to live and die in Dixie.
Away, away, away down south in Dixie.
Away, away, away down south in Dixie.

"Dixie" was, by many accounts, written by Daniel Decatur Emmett, a black minstrel singer born in Ohio, who also wrote "Turkey in the Straw" and "Blue Tail Fly." One narrative has it that on a cold and icy New York morning in 1859, the show manager asked Emmett to write a lively tune that people could whistle in the streets. Emmett imagined how pleasant it must be in the land south of the Mason-Dixon line at that very moment and so scribbled out, "Oh, I wish I was in the land of cotton / Old times there are not forgotten." Dixie was popular throughout the country; it was played at Jefferson Davis's inauguration and was a favorite of Abraham Lincoln's. At the president's request, a band played the song as he stood on the balcony of the White House on the evening of the South's surrender in 1865. But in 1861 the song had become the war anthem of the South. Confederate soldiers loved to march to a quick-step version. In 1948 it became the theme song of the Dixiecrats, the breakaway Southern Democrats.

In 1997, Robert Khayat, the new chancellor and himself a Mississippi native and Ole Miss football star, in effect banned the display of the flag at the stadium. He survived a nasty backlash, and the ban survived a court challenge. (Oddly, financial giving to the university increased after the ban.) In 2003, he banned Colonel Reb from the stadium, which earned an equally virulent response from alumni and others, including one anonymous package containing panties and a bra. (Khayat, who is wildly popular with students, faculty, and alumni, also oversaw the creation of the William Winter Institute for Racial Reconciliation and the construction of a memorial honoring James Meredith. Under his leadership, the first presidential debate of 2008 was held at Ole Miss. On January 9, 2009, Khayat announced his intention to retire at the end of the school year.)

But Khayat let "Dixie" alone. Though he explained that it was a First Amendment issue, one suspects that he knew exactly where the line was and that "Dixie" was on the right side of the line. The version played in the Grove and in the stadium before the national anthem varies from the one written by Emmett. Sometimes referred to as "From Dixie with Love," it combines "Dixie" with "The Battle Hymn of the Republic." In this version, after "Look away, look away, Dixie Land," the words shift to "Glory, glory, hallelujah." After the third repetition, when the words are supposed to be "His truth . . . shall . . . make . . . you . . . free," the stadium shouts out, "The South . . . shall . . . rise . . . again!" At homes games, Elvis often sings along with the crowd on the large scoreboard screen.

On this cool morning the day after Thanksgiving, the Grove is heavily populated with partiers by 10 o'clock. Collecting under the broad sea of standard-issue tents are gatherings of every sort: alumni, students, townspeople, fraternal organizations, neighbors, and, of course, families. It's not unusual for one tent to be made up of family members who have attended Ole Miss, going back three generations and spreading out to third cousins. Hospitality is rampant; if you stop to talk, you are quickly invited in to eat and drink. If you admit you're from the North, your welcome is even warmer, although caution flickers behind the friendly eyes, less you be a *Mississippi Burning*–type Yankee who won't give Mississippi a chance.

The scene is entirely civilized. There are no Confederate flags anywhere to be seen—not on blankets, shirts, vests, hats, tents, car windows, cheeks, or foreheads—but there is lots of red and blue, the school colors, long suspected of having been copied from the Stars and Bars, although according to one account, the crimson was copied from Harvard and the navy blue from Yale. There are no gray kepi caps, no sashes with the Stars and Bars. On the side of one tent is stenciled, "Old Times Here Are Not Forgotten," and on another, "Look Away, Dixie Land." And Colonel Reb has survived his banishment from the stadium: he appears on the backs of canvas chairs and tent flaps, although as depicted he seems more of a cartoon character than a former Confederate officer or slave owner. Still, symbols are symbols. It's a white man's party. Few blacks, other than ticket sellers, are seen in the aisles or under the tents. You hear it said that there are still two universities in Oxford: the University of Mississippi and Ole Miss. True or not, not very many of the thousands of black students and alumni are at the party.

Inside the stadium, the house is fired up. The team, about 70 percent black, is warming up on the field. The cheerleaders, all but four of whom are white, are warming up the audience. Unlike the MSU Bulldog cheerleaders, who are dressed in the traditional skirts and sweaters, Ole Miss cheerleaders are wearing red cocktail dresses with spaghetti straps. Slender, vivacious, hair shining brightly even under the cloudy sky, they will remain uncovered as the afternoon cools, and the sky begins to drizzle. Although the colonel has made his way into the stadium on blankets and chairs brought in by fans, there is not a sign or hint of the Stars and Bars or any other symbol of the Old South. It could be Notre Dame versus USC, except that here you could easily bump into a man spitting tobacco juice into a paper cup or on the cement between his feet. And except when, after playing the alma mater, the band, made up mainly, it seems, of tubas, trumpets, trombones, and huge cymbals, breaks into "Dixie." Out come not tiny flags but a sea of pom-poms in the school's blue and red, which are pushed out in a kind of gentle Atlanta Braves chop as the fans enthusiastically sing along. Cheering starts when the "Battle Hymn" verse begins, and there is a brief pause before the stadium as one voice sings out, "The South shall rise again!" The cheering faces might carry a wisp of the old defiance, but it seems more a matter of sentiment than philosophy. It's like, "Hey, we're still Ole Miss here today. Ain't it fun?" Still standing, hats off, the crowd sings along with "The Star Spangled Banner," which warrants, when it's finished, a louder roar of approval than did "Dixie."

Scouts from the Capitol One, Peach, and Cotton bowls are in the stands, and if Ole Miss wins in style, the team could play on national TV on New Year's Day, like it used to in the old days. With its new coach, Houston Nutt, formerly of Arkansas, at the helm, Ole Miss takes charge from the opening kickoff and pounds the Bulldogs mercilessly. The quarterback completes his first nine passes for 117 yards and two touchdowns. At the end of the first quarter, the Rebels are up 24 to nothing. The quarterback throws a seventy-two-yard scoring pass to make it 31–0 at halftime. The defense smacked the Bulldog quarterback on nine of his first ten pass attempts and intercepted two of his first five passes.

When the Rebels gain ten or more yards in a series, the announcer calls out, "First down," and the fans cry out, "Ole Miss!" At the beginning of the fourth quarter, the audience sings along as the band plays "I Saw the Light." The crowd is enjoying the humbling of its rival the way any football crowd in America would—and is perhaps more civil about it than many would be. There are occasional good-natured calls of "Go back to your cow pastures," referring to Mississippi State's agricultural setting in Starkville, but nothing untoward happens—until late in the third quarter, when an intoxicated older man in jeans and dirty windbreaker stands and begins shouting for the Rebels to "Hit 'em a lick! Hit 'em a lick!" After an Ole Miss score, a black MSU player gets in position to return a punt, and the man yells out, "You're going to have to paint that ball like a watermelon for him to catch it!" Dead silence. Maybe others in the audience want to chuckle but don't; maybe others want to tell the man to sit down and shut up but don't. Even if you're a modern-day Mississippian, there's really nothing much to do about it; a scene would only enlarge the insult. One woman close by finally mutters, "There's ignorant people everywhere."

The Rebels continue to work over the Bulldogs. The MSU quarterback is knocked out of the game twice, once with a sprained shoulder and again with a laceration on his face. The Ole Miss defense dominates the Bulldogs back-field, scoring a record eleven sacks. Mississippi State rushes for minus fifty-one yards and gains a total of thirty-seven yards, less than the forty-five points scored by Ole Miss.

When the final gun sounds, the crowd pours out onto the field. Players grab the Egg Bowl trophy—an egg-shaped football made of gold perched on a wood stand—and parade it joyously around the field. A massive black defensive tackle waves a large Ole Miss flag—a tall red *M* trimmed in white on a blue background—in the center of the field to roars of approval. On the field, white fans hug black players twice their size. Those still in the stands stay cheering and clapping for a long time, letting the pain of old losses ebb away. Balls of cotton rain down from above. (It had to be cotton.) A tall, black defensive end holds the trophy high over his head and trots around the field, pumping it to the screaming fans, finally coming to a stop in front of the Ole Miss band in the stands. Up rise the trumpets, up rise the trombones, the tubas, and the cymbals, and on cue the band swings into the sweet slow beginning of "Dixie": "Oh, I wish I was in the land of cotton." The crowd sings, waving its pom-poms; the band sways; the cheerleaders in their red dresses kick out and cheer; the player, now assisted by others, pushes the golden egg even higher into the blurry gray sky. When the crowd sings, "The South shall rise again!" the whole afternoon peaks in a strange but satisfying explosion.

Two days later, the coach of the vanquished Mississippi State Bulldogs, the only black coach in the SEC, is fired. In Mississippi, as the saying goes, you can't win for losing.

CHAPTER 47

When you finally leave Mississippi, besides feeling a little sad, you realize the effect the place has had on you. The paradoxes, the inconsistencies, the ironies, and the contradictions have begun to seem strangely normal. You've come to see why giants such as William Faulkner, Eudora Welty, Walker Percy, Shelby Foote, Richard Wright, Richard Ford, Tennessee Williams, and Willie Morris—not to mention Robert Johnson, Muddy Waters, and B.B. King—have sprung from this tortured soil; you see that maybe it's because of the need to reconcile suffering with kindness, inhumanity with compassion, ugliness with beauty, both within the land and within themselves, that they sprung from here. Faulkner, the great critic of and participant in the Mississippi drama, is quoted as having said once in a drunken ramble, "If I have to choose between the United States and Mississippi, then I'll choose Mississippi."

Percy and Williams didn't grow up in a one-beat culture, where values seemed to line up square on; nothing in Mississippi lines up square on. What seems true one day seems otherwise the next. In the midst of it all, you find in the inhabitants a deep, abiding love for the soil itself, across racial lines, which comes with a sometimes suffocating sense of the past. You have to develop a personality wide enough, itself inconsistent enough, almost crazy enough, to contain it all. The native writes about it; he sings about it; he defends it; he moves away. But he comes back. It's always home.

David Halberstam's first job out of Harvard was working as a reporter for a paper in West Point, a small town in the piney hills of East Mississippi. He gave the state a hard time, referring to the rednecks as "peckerwoods," a not uncommon appellation, but in one reflective column, he wrote that he believed America would never be whole until Mississippi became part of it.

Mississippi is not where it was forty-five years ago; it's not where it was five years ago. You can't say where it is, or even what it is, for certain, but it seems fair to say that Mississippi is probably in a more intense state of cultural evolution than any other place in the country. The much-feared union of poor whites and poor blacks is finally gaining traction, and educated blacks flood the workforce. Gov. Haley Barbour not long ago signed legislation requiring the teaching of civil rights history in Mississippi schools. You still come across the old beliefs—that whites are fundamentally smarter than blacks—and when you see kids at recess in grade school and in class at Ole Miss segregating themselves by race, you wonder if maybe the dual society of "us and them" will always remain, in one form or another.

But there is no denying that in spite of the antipathy, if not the animosity, of the rest of the country, Mississippi is steadily making progress. It will never be as if the past didn't happen, and there will never be a present free of the past, but when one glimpses over the horizon, as James Meredith does, one can see the possibility of a type of racial reconciliation unknown in the rest of the country, perhaps even the rest of the world. As Mississippi's past might be its eternal burden, it might also be its liberation, and ours as well.

Myrlie Evers, wife of Medgar Evers, wrote these words for inscription on the James Meredith Memorial at Ole Miss: "Yes, Mississippi was, but Mississippi is, and we are proud of what we've become." On the same memorial are inscribed the words of Meredith himself:

> Always without fail, regardless of the number of times I enter Mississippi, it creates within me feelings that I've felt no other time. Joy. Hope. Love. I have always felt that Mississippi belongs to me, and one must love what is his. .

There is no underlying grid of principles or ideas, no unifying theory or distillable truth to uncover that which is Mississippi; there are only observations and hypotheses and tentative insights. Legendary civil rights activist Robert Moses, who directed Freedom Summer in Mississippi, commented, "When you're not in Mississippi, it's not real, and when you're there, the rest of the world isn't real." You think of this when you're leaving, and you feel it when you're returning after a few months' absence. The place has begun strangely to feel like home, and yet you know it never could be. Only those born here can call it home. But if you bump into someone in the elevator or on the street, you know there'll be a sincere apology, even if it was your fault. If you mention where you're from, you know the look of concern that will cross the Mississippian's face. You can say almost anything you want about Mississippi, and there'll be some truth to it. But the opposite will also most likely be true. You've come to accept this fundamental irreconcilability as the sole truth of the place.

Epilogue

The drama of the trial of James Ford Seale, like the drama of Mississippi, seems like a play that will never end. The curtain drops, only to rise again, just as the theater has darkened. On November 14, 2008, the Fifth Circuit Court of Appeals pulled the ropes. On appeal by the government, the court decided to review the case en banc, meaning the entire panel of eighteen judges would review the matter de novo, something it rarely does. Despite Nester's efforts to have her client released on bond pending the outcome of the appeal, Seale remained incarcerated in the federal prison in Terre Haute. On June 5, 2009, the eighteen judges of the Fifth Circuit split nine to nine on the issue of whether the prosecution was barred by the statute of limitations. A tie goes to the government: the original conviction was reinstated and the case remanded to the three-judge panel to hear the other issues raised on the initial appeal.

Meanwhile, the hunt continues: not long after Seale's conviction, the Justice Department announced that it was taking a look at one hundred cold civil rights cases in the South, thirty of which are in Mississippi. Little has come of that effort so far, but after years of delay, on September 24, 2008, Congress finally passed, and the President signed into law, the Emmett Till Unsolved Civil Rights Crime Act, which provides $10 million for the Justice Department and the FBI to investigate and prosecute unsolved civil rights murders from the 1960s. Prosecutor Paige Fitzgerald will head the government's efforts.

On January 2, 2009, Ole Miss played Texas Tech in the Cotton Bowl in Dallas. Ole Miss last played here in 2004, when, under the guidance of Eli Manning (son of deified Archie and brother of traitorous Peyton, who left to play for Tennessee), the Rebels defeated Oklahoma State 31–28. On this day, a record 89,000 people were in attendance for the seventy-third and final game of the Cotton Bowl; 30,000 Ole Miss fans had made the pilgrimage to Dallas, and they sat in a block in their red and blue sweaters and canvas chairs bearing the image of the dyspeptic Colonel Reb. They were aching to finish their 2008 comeback by whipping seventh-ranked Texas Tech, who, coming in at 11–1, had been picked by almost everyone to win.

The weather was warm and sunny, like a spring day. In pregame ceremonies, competing high school bands on the field played "The Star Spangled Banner." The Rebel fans yelled out their defiant chant on cue:

> *Hotty toddy*
> *Gosh Almighty*
> *Who the hell are we*
> *Flim Flam Bim Bam*
> *Ole Miss, by damn.*

And another one, not as unfriendly as it sounds: "We're going to beat the hell out of you."

After fumbling and falling behind by 14–0, the twenty-fifth-ranked Rebels unleashed an explosive offense and led at halftime 24–21. When the Rebels put the game away with a touchdown in the fourth quarter, the Ole Miss band broke into an abbreviated and triple-time version of the original "Dixie." Hearing the refrain, announcer Pat Summerall explained to the audience that the song was "Down in Dixie," or at least he thought that was the name of it. "It is now," his sidekick remarked and predicted how happy everyone was sure to be in "Oxford Dixieland" that night.

Many Texas fans began leaving the stadium at the beginning of the fourth quarter, just as the Ole Miss band played "I've Seen the Light." When the game ended with Ole Miss 47 and Texas Tech 34, the stadium pretty much belonged to the 30,000 Rebel fans, who stayed and cheered and roared as Houston Nutt accepted the trophy and the players held the golden football above their head, as they had the golden egg a few weeks earlier, and pranced and danced and hoisted each other and cheerleaders on their shoulders and pumped fists of victory in the air.

It was as if heaven rained down on the stadium that afternoon. On Mississippi. The Rebels were back; Ole Miss was back—you might not love us, but you've got to respect us. Almost an hour later, when only the faithful remained, when the lights and the cameras had been turned off and the warmth of the autumn sun was fading from the field, and the players and the fans had descended to a calmer level of tumult, the band sucked in a deep breath of cool Texas air and played "From Dixie with Love." This time the beginning slow rhythm of "Dixie" seemed almost mournful, as if reliving the painful loss of an earlier game or a long-ago war, and when the band swung into "The Battle Hymn of the Republic," the great abolitionist hymn, the crowd seems to cheer even louder, seemingly at the notion of Union, or of One Heartbeat, as Houston Nutt had described the Ole Miss spirit. And finally, when the band blew back fast and full blast into the final strains of "Dixie," the excitement seemed suddenly to shift to next year, to the future.

AUTHOR'S NOTE

I became interested in Mississippi long before James Ford Seale was indicted for conspiracy and kidnapping in 2007. The ensuing trial, however, provided the lens, or perhaps the framework, for exploring Mississippi's culture. I attended the preliminary hearings and the trial itself, and spent nights, weekends, and months afterward traveling the state, talking not only to participants in the events of this drama but to ordinary Mississippians as well. I soon confirmed what I had suspected from the beginning: that the mystery of this deeply conflicted place would be far beyond my ability to fully illuminate. Nonetheless, I read stacks of books and articles on the history of Mississippi and the current social, economic, and racial climates in the state. I visited libraries and archives. I interviewed many of the participants in the trial drama, and I interviewed ordinary black and white Mississippians in their homes, at their jobs, and in their schools across the state. In presenting what I found, I did not seek to present a new, complete picture of Mississippi as much as I sought to peel away the layers of perception and challenge the old images and stereotypes.

Requiem for a Nun was Faulkner's fifteenth book and was a sequel to an earlier novel, *Sanctuary*. The title of my book, and perhaps his best-known quote, is taken from an exchange between two characters. The woman, Mrs. Gowan Stevens, previously Temple Drake, has an unsavory past, involving promiscuity and perjury in a murder trial, which she tries to leave behind. Her husband's uncle, Gavin Stevens, refers to something Temple had done in the past, eliciting the following exchange.

TEMPLE: Mrs. Gowan Stevens did.
STEVENS: Temple Drake did. Mrs. Gowan Stevens is not even fighting in this class. This is Temple Drake's.
TEMPLE: Temple Drake is dead.
STEVENS: The past is never dead. It's not even past.

While Mrs. Stevens, or Temple Drake, later concludes that her past has damned and doomed her, Stevens suggests that the past is like a promissory note: while you might be able to pay it off in an orderly manner, it can equally easily foreclose on you without warning.

Mississippi's hope is that its sin is not mortal, that its past can be redeemed before the note comes due.

ACKNOWLEDGMENTS

The credit for this effort, such as it may be, is rightfully spread among many people. I bear the most gratitude to Hulya O'Brien, a woman of strong spirit and limitless patience who not only spent endless hours on the manuscript in its early stages, but also provided loving support through every step of the research and writing of the book. Tom Pace mixed wonderfully, as only he can, the invaluable roles of counselor, friend, and critic. I was also very fortunate to have the spiritual wisdom of Jane Kopp, who understood and supported the vision from the beginning. My nephew Mark MacLean raised questions and concerns throughout the process that had to be addressed, and the book is far better for it.

I would like to thank my agent, Paul Bresnick, a true author's agent, whose caring and careful hand found the right home for the book. I also would like to acknowledge my editor at Perseus, Brandon Proia, whose thoughtful ideas and incisive comments—always graciously given—improved the manuscript immensely from beginning to end, as well as project editor Sandra Beris for bringing the finished product together in such fine form.

It is impossible to thank all of the people in Mississippi who contributed to this book. Mississippians are each as unique as the state itself, but most were willing to dig deep into their memories and share their thoughts and feelings about their home state. Their insights were often profound and wonderfully articulated. In addition to those many Mississippians mentioned in the book, I would like to especially express my gratitude for the contributions of Avery Rollins, a former FBI agent and native Mississippian, and Dave Molina, staff member of the William Winter Institute for Racial Reconciliation.

I am also grateful to Stephen White, Tom Kanan, Susie Hupp, Deb Mickelson, and many others who in different ways have supported my writing efforts over the years.

This book is dedicated to my older brother, Mike MacLean. Mike was a wise and steadying force in my life, as he was in the lives of countless others. He lived his life with integrity and compassion, and he unfailingly and unselfishly supported those around him on their journeys. Mike read the manuscript with care and made valuable suggestions, many of which are now evident in the book. In here, as elsewhere, his spirit continues.